Murder
for
Profit

Murder
for
Profit

by William Bolitho

 TIME Reading Program Special Edition

TIME INCORPORATED / NEW YORK

TIME-LIFE BOOKS
EDITOR *Norman P. Ross*
TEXT DIRECTOR *William Jay Gold*
ART DIRECTOR *Edward A. Hamilton*
CHIEF OF RESEARCH *Beatrice T. Dobie*
ASSISTANT TEXT DIRECTOR *Jerry Korn*

EDITOR, TIME READING PROGRAM *Max Gissen*
RESEARCHER *Ann S. Lang*
DESIGNER *Lore Levenberg*

PUBLISHER *Jerome S. Hardy*
GENERAL MANAGER *John A. Watters*

TIME MAGAZINE
EDITOR *Roy Alexander*
MANAGING EDITOR *Otto Fuerbringer*
PUBLISHER *Bernhard M. Auer*

COVER DESIGN *Austin Briggs*

Contents

Editors' Preface

EVERY YEAR, THOUSANDS OF MURDER STORIES ARE printed, some of them accounts of actual slayings, others fictional mysteries. Amid all this literary mayhem, there have been surprisingly few thoughtful examinations of the state of mind that impels men to kill in cold blood. In particular, few writers have ever tried to probe the psychology of one puzzling kind of criminal: the man who slays for personal profit—sometimes for profit so trivial that it scarcely seems worth the trouble, let alone the risk.

It is this task of explaining the apparently inexplicable that William Bolitho undertook when he wrote *Murder for Profit*. Bolitho grappled with the incomprehensible in the only possible way: with a cool detachment and an inexorable logic that have gained the book a reputation over the years as a tour de force of common-sense analysis. As Dr. Fredric Wertham, the distinguished psychiatrist, notes in his new introduction to this special edition, the book is also a classic portrayal of murder's relationship to the society in which it occurs. It is, in addition, a major literary achievement—a magnificently written narrative, worth reading just for the skillful handling of its ghoulish stories.

Bolitho, in the words of his fervent admirer Heywood Broun, was a "leader of journalistic exploration, deep into the human heart and mind," a man who was "far more interested in the explanation than in the event." In this casebook Bolitho leads the reader, calmly and dispassionately, straight into the minds of his killers. By the careful use of surmise and by adroit reconstruction—"Only imaginative curiosity is necessary," writes Bolitho, "and as unsqueamish nerves as possible"—he exposes the motives that made his ghastly protagonists turn off the part of their minds that listened to society's injunction not to kill.

Bolitho chose a mixed (though psychologically related) bag of killers for his analysis, and in the book he characterizes them with a skill that makes their homicidal behavior seem entirely credible, if shocking. There are Burke and Hare, the Edinburgh grave robbers: "If Burke was a dog, an ill-bred country mongrel that any shepherd would shoot, Hare's appearance had somewhat of the devilry or the insane levity of a wolf." This disparate pair and their harridan women gradually evolved a seemingly foolproof way to broaden their supply of cadavers for the city's medical schools.

There is Jean-Baptiste Troppmann, an ambitious and irascible maniac with "a fair education, an unbounded will, a profoundly rooted sense of grievance," who stood waiting, "yellow and spidery," to kill a mother and her six children (he made some of the younger children wait their turn while he disposed of the rest of the family). He wanted to clear his title to some money; it belonged to the father of the family, Troppmann's best friend, whom he had killed some weeks before.

There is G. J. Smith, whose "self-compassion, self-pity, wakened by what self-knowledge of wretchedness we do not know, sucked the meaning out of every existence but his own." Smith fancied himself a financial manipulator but had to insure and slay lonely women to provide capital for his interminable and meaningless transactions.

There is Desiré Landru, the latter-day Bluebeard and inspirer of dozens of novels, stories and dramas, in whose dreadful exploits a France ravaged by World War I finally discovered some killings it could bear to discuss. "Returned soldiers . . . followed with delighted recollection . . . the accounts of Landru's crimes. This host, back from killing, or suddenly relieved from the fear of being killed, with the taste of despair still under their tongues, learnt with a roar that a little funny man had all these years behind their backs been conducting a private war of his own, earnestly mimicking theirs, even to the casualties."

And there is Fritz Haarmann, the "ogre of Hanover," who "bettered the satanic economies of Smith, and was damned in deeper erotics than Landru." Calmly and in a workmanlike fashion, Haarmann killed some 27 boys to sell their clothes and pocket trinkets—and perhaps their flesh.

In his studies of these six and their appalling crimes, Bolitho looks for differences—in temperament, motive,

technique. But he also finds provocative similarities, leading him to ponder whether "the modern mass-murderer,
like the Industrial Man of which he is a fascinating variety,
has evolved into a distinct type." Bolitho finds some evidence to support the existence of such a type:

> It certainly is a temptation to follow up such clues as
> the early family discords . . . all had in their lives
> . . . their youthful hate of their fathers. Then there is
> that remarkable uniformity in their daily occupations.
> . . . All, too, were men with . . . a taste for self-im-
> provement. In their inner life, all were day-dreamers. All
> seemed not only to suffer but actively to cultivate a
> peculiar professional deformation, a point of view which
> in many ways bore a queer resemblance to that of men
> of law and business. . . . All were devoted family men;
> all, compared with their *milieu,* sober and methodical in
> their habits.

In addition, Bolitho finds all of these men compelled
by what he calls the Law of Repetition: if a profitable
homicide works once they do it just the same way again—
Burke and Hare go on stuffing bodies into herring barrels,
Smith drowns his inamoratas in their bathtubs—until finally the compulsive reiteration betrays them. He finds
them all peculiarly drawn from those professions of society where things, even lives, tend to lose any value except a commercial one. Two of his killers are second-hand
dealers who have turned to dealing, at second-hand, in
people. He finds all of them afflicted with a turn of mind
which builds elaborate mechanical schemes—complex and
heavy, like the early engines of the Victorian era which
generated most of these crimes—in which killing was the

crucial cog, in theory kicking into action the machine which would obediently grind out a profit in return for the invested deaths.

There are similarities aplenty. Were Bolitho a glib writer faced with this evidence, one concerned merely with the orderly presentation of a neat package, he would, perhaps, fasten on these extraordinary likenesses and in fact generate a model slayer. Bolitho refuses to take the obvious way. "However tempting it would be to reunite all these characters and make a mass-murderer type distinguishable from the rest of humanity . . . I am convinced that it would be a great stupidity . . . not only are each of these characteristics extremely common . . . but such a breed is an inevitable, if unintentional, by-product of the modern industrial society."

Instead, Bolitho deals with his killers as individuals, in the process stripping their motives down to the bare bone. Of Smith and his relations with one of his victims, he says: "He does the shopping and insists on her staying in bed late, so that he can hate her," and "he carefully concealed from her the way he liked things done, so that she could offend him." Haarmann he calls "an ideal soldier, obedient, full of esprit de corps, delighting in every insipid detail." Of Landru he says "he was a shabby, bowed little man, fitted for peddling or any form of selling in which pity besides business has to matter. As to his manner, that is different. His speech was highly persuasive to a certain class of women and young persons, for he had a great deal of calm, always based himself on the most assimilable form of reason, Law, and ornamented every statement with

technical words which gave . . . an appearance of great
dignity. When in argument, he would not allow the contradictor to state his own case, but he would do it for him
quickly and fairly, then demolish it, gravely and sometimes
with an expression of sympathetic regret."

Bolitho wrote incisively and with detachment about
society and its ways of taking lives, and the reason may be
that he had once nearly lost his own life at the hands of society and had had plenty of time to think about it. In 1916,
as a British soldier on the Somme, he was buried in a trench
by a shell burst. Fifteen men with him died, but he was en-
tombed alive. Ultimately he was exhumed, but he stayed
unconscious for several weeks and in the hospital for a
year. He was not a writer then but a 26-year-old knocka-
bout. Born in 1890 in South Africa as William Bolitho
Ryall, he had been a newsboy, a laborer, a stoker on a British liner and a student of metaphysics before he went to
France to fight and nearly to die. It was not until after the
war that he turned to writing, first as Paris correspond-
ent for the Manchester *Guardian,* then for the New
York *World.*

In 1928 Bolitho came to New York and started writing a three-times-a-week column for the *World.* His work
there, some of which was collected in a posthumous book
called *Camera Obscura* in 1930, shows the same concern
with motive, rather than surface manifestations, that dis-
tinguishes *Murder for Profit.* Alexander Woollcott, trying
to describe Bolitho's predilection for showing why things
work rather than just how, wrote that Bolitho "contem-
plated the human pageant with unique detachment. . . . To
hear Bolitho talk was to listen to one who himself dwelt

outside of time. . . . [He was an] obscure young observer as interested, as skeptical and as detached as the man from Mars."

That was Woollcott talking about the Bolitho of 1918. But Bolitho did not long stay obscure. Broun came to call him "the most brilliant journalist of our time." He began to write books, among them *Leviathan* (1924), *Italy under Mussolini* (1926) and most notably *Twelve Against the Gods* (1929), a study of 12 adventurers, ranging from Casanova to Woodrow Wilson, in whom he found common causes and conceits much like the ones he had earlier distilled from the killers of *Murder for Profit.* His books gradually bought him enough time so that he could spend part of the year writing still others. He was working on no fewer than six and had just finished a play, *Overture,* when he died, suddenly and tragically, in June 1930. He died in a hospital at Avignon, a victim of the mistaken judgment of an obscure French physician who let a case of appendicitis go to peritonitis and death. He was just 39.

—THE EDITORS OF TIME

Introduction

STORIES ABOUT MURDER, FICTIONAL OR NONFICTIONAL, fascinate us. Why? Many a publisher, many an educator, has asked himself that question. I think that fundamentally the answer is not very difficult to find. Murder is a clear-cut event. Whether or not we find the corpse or the murderer or the motive, we know that whenever a murder has occurred, two (at least two) human beings have clashed with an irrevocable result. So much in our life and literature is unclear and ambiguous; murder is certain. But if we want to understand it, it is always a challenge. My own studies indicate that its main characteristic is that it breaks through the routine of our life, and that it always has this breakthrough effect on two levels: the psychological and the social.

The principal characters in a murder—the person who commits it, the person who tries to find the murderer, and the people who have to decide what should be done with him—all present interesting psychological problems. Modern dynamic clinical psychiatry has taught us a great deal about motives, inhibitions, internal impulses, emotional crises. What we have learned from the psychopathology of minor emotional disorders has helped to throw a light on violent deeds, and conversely what we may glean from murder cases in their stark and exaggerated simplicity can help us to understand the more obscure details of harmless neurotic difficulties.

But however deep our depth psychology of the unconscious is, it remains superficial if it leaves out the objective social conditions under which people—all people—live. The pressures come not only from within but also from outside. Every murder case, especially if it comes to trial, throws a searchlight on the society in which it occurs, and we become aware of a fixed moment in social history. There is currently an overemphasis on the irrational and the individually morbid; this leads to an evasion of social responsibility and to the nonrecognition and therefore perpetuation of evil social conditions. In this, psychiatry, although it can do an immense amount of good, can be put to evil uses as well. Many homicide cases have been so snowed under by psychiatric speculation that their social meaning, without which prevention is impossible, has become obscured.

The social meaning of murder does not escape William Bolitho. His *Murder for Profit* is a classic. That term may have different connotations. It may mean an excellent work that is decorative on the shelf but a little removed from our current concerns. Or it may designate a book which, though written some time ago, is so well done and so rich in content that it still has the most serious implications for later generations. *Murder for Profit* is such a book. It can be read for pleasure, entertainment and enlightenment, but in addition it is a book of warning. When it was first published, in 1926, this warning was not heeded. It applies even more today.

Bolitho's great merit is that while he does not in any way neglect the psychological background of the mass murderers he describes, he also takes pains to demonstrate their intimate relationship to society. He does not merely show the immediate social environment, but places the cases in their historical setting. What, you may ask, has the infamous rule of Louis Napoleon to do with an individual murderer like Troppmann? To be sure, Bolitho does not give us all the answers, but he indicates some of them—the politics of the day, their socio-economic foundations and what he calls the general weather of society. He gives us enough hints for further thought and study.

You may ask further: What good is it for the author to stress this sociological-historical dimension? The answer, to be read between the lines of Bolitho's book, is simple. We sorely need this social setting for prediction and prevention. A mass murderer used to be a man who killed maybe four or five, or even 10 or 20 people. Mass killing now is more likely to involve millions.

Perhaps the most important part of *Murder for Profit* is the story of the mass murderer Fritz Haarmann, who flourished in Germany in the post-World War I period.

Haarmann, it is now established, was in all probability a recruiter for the secret Reichswehr; he definitely served as a political undercover agent and he was employed by the police to hunt homosexuals. The last-named capacity gave him the opportunity to approach and threaten young boys, use them sexually and kill them. For years, although many complaints were received, the police failed to stop him.

I find a strange and compelling parallel between this failure of the police to track down a mass murderer, because he seemed to be engaged in what was considered legitimate business, and certain cases in my own professional experience. I have psychiatrically examined several mass murderers. Many of the child murders committed by a man named Albert Fish, for example, could have been prevented if there had been more action by the authorities —psychiatric, police and judicial—who had dealt with him repeatedly during the period when he was killing. Cannibalism was an issue in both the case of Haarmann and that of Fish. In the case of Haarmann the cannibalism was denied or played down. In the Fish case the cannibalism was dismissed by a district attorney's psychiatric expert with the astonishing statement, made under oath, that "there is no accounting for taste." It is more than a rhetorical statement that part of the responsibility for Fish's mass murders, the social responsibility, rested on the authorities—that is, on all of us.

Russel Crouse, co-producer of *Arsenic and Old Lace,* commenting on this Bolitho essay, once remarked that Haarmann was "a forerunner of the many who were to blossom under Nazi nurturing." Indeed he was. Even the corporate killing of Murder, Inc., seems trivial in the light of the Nazi mass murders. Good reporter that he is, Bolitho mentions that one journalist present, Theodor Lessing, was expelled from the Haarmann courtroom because he reported too frankly on the ramifications of the evidence. I have done some research on Theodor Lessing. What I found makes this introduction to Bolitho's book also a postscript. Lessing not only recognized the significance of the Haarmann case but wrote about other German political happenings which led up to the Nazi regime. The Nazis never forgave him. He had to flee Germany in 1933. The Nazis found him in exile in Prague and an SS man murdered him there. In the same way that Lessing's expulsion from the Haarmann courtroom, reported by Bolitho, was an omen, Lessing's murder by the SS man outside Germany was a portent of things to come. Bolitho's writing was prophetic.

The Nazi murders, in their turn, foreshadowed the cloud of violence under which we now live. We are already counting in tens of millions the prospective casualties of the next world war. Moreover, younger and younger children are daily committing brutal acts of violence like those presented to them unrelentingly in the mass media.

The warning we may read in Bolitho's book is this: The mass phenomenon of murder, if we follow all its ramifications, is no longer an isolated phenomenon. We are all implicated. We have lost one right irrevocably— the right to be surprised. That is as true of the latest murder of a little girl on the roof of a tenement in New York as it is of the assassination of a President. The violence of our era, of which mass murder is one facet, is a new moral problem for the philosophers to work out. But the prevention of violence is everybody's business.

—FREDRIC WERTHAM, M.D.

Murder

for

Profit

Race de Cain, ton supplice
Aura-t-il jamais une fin?

— LES FLEURS DU MAL.

THE STUDY OF PROFESSIONAL, OR MASS-MURDERERS AS A class has seldom been attempted, though each of these men as he is discovered and tied up for extermination is a universal interest at the time, that often to the disgust of moralists outlasts the fame of dull worth. The documentation for such a study is of a peculiar kind. Each murderer usually has his hack-literature, and as the bad paper wears out, his popular legend, which though in general only concerned with the stage setting of the man, is worth attention. There is also to be found sometimes a more sophisticated material. De Quincey's fugue on the ghastly yellow silk dressing-gown of Sailor Williams, one of the minor mass-murderers, has enticed many later essayists to treat of such persons, indiscriminately with mere occasional homicides, in a tone which is often humorous. In England this genre of writing, especially since Wilde connived at it, has definitely made murder, along with the amateur study of religious rites and ceremonies, and sexual aberrations, one of the subjects allowed to interest cultured men after dinner. But out of this class of essay (which often survives in the preface) has grown the excellently interesting custom of reprinting verbatim reports of celebrated murder trials. These naturally vary in quality. The literary value of some of these crystallisations of emotion and life, their natural drama, is sometimes close to that of our anonymous ballads, and often superior, in smack and tang, to those many artless autobiographies in which our national literature is rich. This interest does not always depend on the personality of the prisoner, nor on the history of his crime, but with the class of witness, the talent of the counsel, and most of all with the atmosphere engendered: that is, principally with the character of the judge. The judge is our chanty-man, the orchestral priest who sets the pitch of the chorus of aboriginal cruelty and fear (society's and the criminal's) that goes up in court in every capital trial. With a word he can whip out of a witness a shuddering phrase that jogs the whole celebration to its metre, like a refrain. With a ruthless order, he can also pin all the talk to a severe string of dates and affirmations, that may save his trial from banality, in its pruned simplicity. The emotional strain depends on the judge. Better a thousand times a moral pedant in such a place, than the witty, loquacious, sophisticated interferer, whose effect is as disastrous as a professor at a folk-dance, and who, at worst, may completely spoil our trial, or at best may only leave for future readers a baroque decoration of his old-fashioned interruptions round the evidence. A murder trial is the celebration of a human sacrifice by suffocation, to which modern men are excited in a crowd by the recital of some bloody deed, whose details awaken hate and fear to which the coming execution is the fore-shadowed, fore-tasted complementary. Everything there, prayers, codes, robes, and bars, is devised to create that hoarse atmosphere in which alone modern men, in a state of peace, can work themselves up to a corporate killing, and to whose terrible reality the witnesses respond so that they speak truthfully and unlock themselves.

It is the closeness of this reality, so close that all can feel her breath, in a trial for murder, and not for the æsthetic interest that her presence engenders—the natural architecture of such ceremonies—that gives the subject its main value. Buried under the accumulations of prejudice, theory, abstraction, or hopelessly mislaid among the strange complexitity of our modern life, the elusive reality of things evades us, yet everlastingly attracts us. But here, in the centre of the strangest and most artificial of all circumstances, the presence is close; its odour and its glitter draw the dull-sensed crowd in swarms. This is the reason for the crowd-tails outside the Old Bailey in season. This is the sensible cause for the thick-topped columns in all newspapers when a great murder trial is in progress. The theatre may rival in the hands of a genius the naïve drama of the courts, though in England at any rate the theatre had dilapidated itself in trying to make our ethics plausible, and the 'real-life' drama has no serious rival. But it is its reality, not its drama, wherein lies the core of the interest of murder. We have a need for the sight of life and death as for salt. We wage-slaves live continually in incompletion and inexplicability; we strain for a sight of stars and mud; we wish to take our bearings and know where we stand. This reality if it spices the meanest affair of *crime passionel,* reeks far and wide in the trial of a wholesale murderer, who has acted not in a fit of rage, but for profit.

Killing and creation are the terminal businesses of life; killing like creation is fenced up to the sky; it has its foundations in the recesses of the spirit. A man who earns his life by death makes us tremble for him, as well as for ourselves. No one can kill with impunity to himself; in that act are roused instincts and pleasures which imperil reason itself. And here step in what humanity has best and most worthy of a hearing, the scientists, with their hands held up in warning. Here the eager hunt for reality must stop, they say, for here madness begins. The criminal is mad; here is the closure of psychological inquiry, as well as the blank-wall of revenge, the blind-alley of the Law.

At any rate we may examine their warrant. The claim of medicine to the murderer as its exclusive property has taken many forms within the past generation. So many forms that one sometimes suspects some extra-scientific, possibly unconscious motive in the persistence; as one hypothesis is found empty, another is built: Lombroso is discarded, but Freud takes his place. At every changing of the guard the pass-word becomes more subtle. We are no longer, since many years, asked to believe that the explanation of all conduct is the dints and bosses of the skull. In its latest form the theory seems to run that madness is not essentially an intellectual but an emotional disorder. The intellect may be unimpaired, though usually the critical faculties are weakened. But even in a deep science, Logic has not lost her rights. This man is mad, because we think he must have felt mad, is not a tolerable proposition, however it is wrapped. In such cases as we shall examine, the doctors have been obliged to grant that there was no obvious intellectual derangement, except from a very high and arbitrarily chosen norm, one which would bar equally the vast majority of our own every-day acts, all our finer ones in any case. That murderers often, even always, make a false reconstruction of the outside world for themselves in which notably they attribute an unreasonable place for their own importance, cannot be accepted as sufficient grounds for the deduction that their physical brain is sick, or whatever other precise sense the alienists, within the narrow range of its legitimate meaning, like to set on the word 'mad.' Before that, and even before the various shades of the term, deranged, weak-minded, irresponsible, and so forth, can be applied confidently, something more than the terribly abstract norm of emotion, reason, conduct hitherto set up, will have to be devised. Ambition, Greed, Selfishness, Vanity, are at least as normal as their contraries, even in acutely stupid forms. These are men, certainly not deranged automata that we will observe; the worst men, not madmen; even on the slightest acquaintance nastily like ourselves. They do not despise in their technique of life any of the anodynes that we 'of the virtue' use against poverty, loneliness, hunger, the contempt of our fellows, or predatory competition. If they very commonly construct for themselves a life-romance, a personal myth in which they are the maltreated hero, which secret is the key of their life, in such comforting day-dreams many an honest man has drugged himself against despair.

The mass-murderer lies to himself. Also, he is often a

good family man. Some criminologists have even made out of this weakness a sensational theory that every bad man has bodily need of one companion in his life. This support for the essential necessity of the system of monogamy is perhaps a too-daring distortion of the commonplace fact that Smith loved his Edith Pegler, Landru his Fernande Segret, Troppmann his mother, and Burke his faithful paramour. Another obvious fact on which less daring theorising has been expended is that the mass-murderer is almost always found to have had dealings, psychological at any rate, with the institution of War. I do not principally mean that he holds the concept of a social war, in which his hand is against society and all fair. That is naturally a usual way of thinking among them, as among any other class of men in an unsheltered corner of this competitive world. There are more subtle connexions between the murderer and war. Curiously often there is a direct history of soldiering. When he tries to explain himself, the murderer invariably appeals to the ethics by which 'the noblest manifestation of a nation in action' is defended. 'In wartime, one kills,' whispered the girl in the Malakoff murder to decide her chicken-hearted lover. '*A la guerre on tue.*' It is on some such plank of doctrine, stolen from the common stock, that the mass-murderer crosses that profound but narrow chasm that separates the theft of property from the theft of life; not always in an ecstatic bound or frensied leap, as the alienists tend to claim.

So, in these and many other curious respects, as you shall see, the mass-murderer bears an interesting resemblance to those with a full right to be called human. The contemplation of the ways and walks of these monsters

among the children of men to which you are invited is
thus neither beneath the attention of a cultured man, nor
will defraud the first bait of Reality which it held out. Here
are no automata, no deranged mechanical marionettes,
such as the doctors endeavour to have us believe, but
terrible flesh and blood, the breed of Cain, whose dramatic
chase is not only one of the most lawful of the deeds of
the community, but whose incursions and ambushes
among the inner streets of our modern cities have given
rise to the most astonishing adventures, which often show
a new light on some very commonplace things. The very
evolution of a mass-murderer is interesting, so like it is in
many curious aspects to our own, though the results have
so remarkable a difference. Only imaginative curiosity is
necessary, and as unsqueamish nerves as possible. Those
which used to serve us in reading the G. H. Q. *communiqués* will amply suffice.

The
Science
of
William
Burke

Up the close and doun the stair,
But and ben with Burke and Hare,
Burke's the butcher, Hare's the thief,
Knox the boy that buys the beef.

—OLD SONG.

THE GENEALOGIES OF MASS-MURDERING MAY GROW BACK, as Voltaire thought, to the first king, priest, and hero. The occupation of profitable homicide may antecede even that of the hunter. But only its modern examples, with the mysteries due to our conscience, manners and economic system come within my scope. A complete study would be almost impossible to dissect from the complication of human history; thus bandits would be hard to disentangle from political history, pirates from empire building, inquisitors from the general history of the progress of science. Many of the most tempting examples belong to a phase of culture that no longer exists; thus the Marquise de Brinvilliers was an aristocrat, and the class is now extinct. The modern mass-murderer, like the Industrial Man of which he is a fascinating variety, has evolved into a distinct type, with his own peculiarities that only vaguely recall his predecessors in social history. The first useful examples are Burke and Hare—William Burke and William Hare.

Both were Irishmen, that is of a race and education rather inferior to the general level in Edinburgh, the city in which they exercised their trade. William Burke was born in Orrey, Tyrone, in 1792. His father was a petty farmer, on leased lands, a condition in his country below that of any pre-revolution Breton peasant. Natural momentum would have made of the boy a half-savage labourer like his companions, with no more originality than in his fashion of standing his liquor. The first seed of the difference in him that was to place him forever in another class, may have entered when his father, against local usage, though a Roman Catholic, placed William as house boy to a Presbyterian minister near by. One cannot expect any much closer account of the boyhood of even the greatest of criminals. But it is known that early contact with two hostile religions often stimulates an intelligence, and so ambition. Henceforth, quite believably because of this accident, William Burke has that restless, scattered wish to better himself which is recorded of most of his peers in crime. They suffer from an itch of ambition, that is neither high nor persistent enough to do anything but bring them to the butt end of half a dozen trades, more paying than those to which they were born, but needing more education and discipline than they possess. Burke, like Smith, like Landru, was an autodidact in all trades as long as he lived, and he had the same nagging anxiety as they about his livelihood. After leaving the Manse, he tried intermittently the discomforts of baking, the long monot-

onies of the weaving craft. He enlisted in the Militia,
where he served seven years, most of them as officer's batman. After discharge, he went to live with his wife and his
three children, in his father's house. After a short stay,
discontented with the prospects, he went for another toxic
dose of the society of his betters as body-servant again. In
a couple of years of this employment, with no abatement of
his restlessness, he returned home. Even in those indigent
surroundings there seems to have been a prize; the sub-
lease of a sheltered potato-patch, which William, momentarily bent on being a farmer, coveted and his father refused. There followed one of those Irish quarrels, in which
the noise does not weaken the bitterness. In 1818, at
twenty-six years old, William abandoned them all, and in
the situation of exile, dangerous for a man of his sort, he
crossed the cold sea to Glasgow.

Here he easily found work as a navvy on the Union
Canal. Pay-envelopes were good; he stuck to pick and
shovel until the job ended. By then he had fallen in with
a doxy named Helen M'Dougal, whom he took over from
a sawyer, and the two wandered over the Lowlands as
masterless man and mistress. In Leith, Burke's itch for self-
improvement broke out again; he induced his landlord to
teach him how to clout shoes, and as the latter's art was
not longer than Burke's power of concentration, when the
couple moved towards Edinburgh, 1817, Burke was in possession of all the smaller secrets of cobbling. The couple
put up at the Beggar's Hotel, an Irish resort, which was
not dubbed in joke. The woman would go out early and
find, or buy, old shoes; at home her man would repair
them, and in the evenings she would hawk them round

the town. To this commerce Burke's versatility led him to add the general pedlary of other discarded goods; old clothes, rabbit- and cat-skins, human hair. He had reached, by no shorter cut than usual, the last station of the unskilled, discontented man, a hundred years before Landru and Haarmann, the jumble trade. There is certainly no quick induction to be drawn as to the morality of dealers at second-hand. Mass-murderers are few, the corporation immense. But men such as Burke—we will later see how other mass-murderers resembled him—wash towards the handling of half-worn-out goods, as fatally as a cork to the shore; there to wait until another tide floats them over into the lonely reach where we find them. But so many coincidences make it worth while to look closer at this business of second-hand dealing, to learn from it what we can of the mechanism of mass-murderers to whom it has so strangely often given a living. The modern economic system is a box with two bottoms. Where the smallest regular business of making and selling goods for consumption ends, begins the vast and incoherent traffic of half-used things. Everything but soft food loses its status gradually, and while its use to its owner is degraded, still is a desirable possession to someone else. So in theory, which, in thrifty towns, as Paris is and Edinburgh was, is carried amazingly near practice, practically every product of our total production is susceptible of two sales, at least. First to its prime user, second to the 'second-hand.'

But this lower, or later, commerce cannot be canalised into shops of speciality as it was in its first sale. There is too great a variety in the goods, condition, their value has degenerated too much for even a distant replica of the mechanism of their first distribution ever to be constructed. So specialisation is infrequent in the commerce at second-hand, especially in the less durable articles, and the element of bargaining, that is of rival estimation of value, is the chief characteristic of the whole trade. To it are inevitably attracted all those waifs of life who have experience, which has brought shrewdness, but lack special knowledge. It is the repository of those who themselves are in a sense second-hand, who have worn out or never fitted their first socket in the social system. Only rarely is a man born into this market, and then he naturally trends towards such specialisation as is possible. If the unskilled labour reservoir receives the waster and, in moral irony, the loafer, towards the traffic in the vast body of once-owned goods filters by gravity the unspecialised intelligence. In the range of this occupation—huge, as is natural in a class only named by a negative—are to be found types as diverse as their wares: the ruined landlord, who deals in last year's cars, the solitary rag, bone and bottle merchant who competes with the municipal incinerator. The mere fact then that the life history of mass-murderers rather often includes a stage in this calling is no slight upon it. Lack of specialisation has brought our subjects to such precarious fields, where they find: (1) fierce competition of interests, where all is haggling; (2) close personal touch with individuals constantly entailed. If out of these two closely related features of this occupation is conceived to arise an increase of the cheat instinct so innate in mankind that it needs no demonstration, with the multiple occasions for its convenient gratification that this huckstering affords, then it is no more wonder the heartless petty swindler, who, I hope to show, is the seed of the mass-murderer, is as happy in this ambiance as a bandit in a forest. Such germinating seed was William Burke in 1818, in the days before he met Hare. He was growing daily in the art of seeing men as material objects revolving round his central reality, as juicy shadows of another creation; to be cheated, used, fought, skinned, abolished when the only need he had come to recognise, the livelihood of William Burke and Helen M'Dougal, required. And these are the first lessons in murder.

The two men are said to have been a lively contrast when they faced each other in court. To Burke's 'down-looking, sleasy look of a dog,' his useless nose, his round, unwrinkled cheeks, his short, thick frame inapt for any gait but a waddle, rose up in clear opposition the fantastic Hare. Hare was a 'spare wretch, grewsome and ghoulish'; he seemed much taller than his partner, all in lines, instead of ill-drawn curves; his face was hollow-ground to a point. Two grey eyes set so far apart that he had difficulty in focusing them, these set in obliquely, under two thick strokes of eyebrows, like a Tartar or a faun. This phantom has constant vivacity, he cannot stand still on his legs, but must be laughing or snapping. He frightened those who saw him when his history was known, but in his former days gave only the impression of a minus-habens, not quite an idiot, but a 'mad Irishman.' If Burke was a dog, an ill-bred country mongrel that on sight any shepherd would shoot, Hare's appearance had somewhat of the devilry or the insane levity of the wolf. Hare's pre-history has even less substance than that of his inseparable partner. We know nothing of him, in fact, until he arrived in

Scotland to work on that same Union Canal, from Glasgow to Edinburgh, which was the humble Eldorado of so many of his wandering countrymen. He was of like race, age, breeding to Burke. Probably Hare himself would have found it difficult to give a more detailed account of the years that had brought him to Log's Boarding House, in the Tanner's Close, where Burke and his M'Dougal had entered as lodgers in 1826. For if the cardinal fault or failing of Burke is an ailing ambition, that characteristic of Hare is a lack of memory. In the mental life of most men there are no free thoughts, for each as it gets up is hooked by the foot in the piled accumulation of the past. Memory, with the background of punishments, fatigues, partings, regrets, breaks our actions, as it hampers all our thoughts and its weight produces the prevalent mood that we call character. On a man like Burke this incubus of the past was especially heavy. He lay always under a permanent weight he had been accumulating since his birth, of hungers, disappointments, frustrations once suffered. He was tongue-tied, and slow in direct consequence. With Hare, though the mechanism of recollection was little impaired—he could remember details of the murders as well as or better than Burke—yet the past had no hold on him.

His actions were sudden and unrelated to such a degree that he found it easy to raise a laugh; his thoughts had the inferior originality of a child. He was ticklish and sudden in his passions, unrepentant and unmalicious, and this lightness compared with the seeming stupidity of Burke brought many into the error of considering him as the real leader of their joint enterprises. In court Hare laughed, whenever his throat tickled, whenever a fly blundered in a pane, even while he was charging himself with nightmares of infamy; so that the judge himself turned pale with rage. The choice of the crowd for lynching would have been Hare, certainly an injustice.

In any association of four persons for an important act, there are bound, of course, to be simple contrasts and likenesses in their persons. Burke was squat and sullen, Hare thin and fantastic. Helen M'Dougal was the sodden remains of a coarse beauty: morose and introspective like her Burke. She was Presbyterian and feared hell by fits and starts. Hare, after the death of Log, the landlord of the boarding-house where he stayed, took up with Log's wife, Margaret Laird, Irishwoman. Like her bully, Mag Hare was lively and vicious, a 'skinny, scranky, wisened jade,' eager with her nails and her kisses. When Log first came to Scotland, he and Maggie Laird worked on the Union Canal, he as small contractor, she after the custom of the Irishry in breeches and man's coat, wheeling a barrow as a common labourer. This was Hare's woman, a virago, as Burke's was a drab.

This quarternion seemingly devised by nature for a symbolical dance of the vices, must naturally in their state and times be observed under the influence of liquor. The heresy of Alcohol as a first cause will make no converts from a study of mass-murder, and meet many rebuffs. Haarmann was unable to drink even a glass of beer, Landru was notoriously abstemious. No one ever saw Smith drunk. A sophist could make more of the thesis of teetotalism as cause for professional murder than the opposite. But in the case of these West Port killers, Irish labourers, living 'in sin,' exiles, it is inevitable that they should have been users of the bottle; and it is of some importance to observe the effects that it had upon them. None of them were besotted, all of them indulged in periodic excesses. When Burke had drunk his capacity, his burden slipped from him. He became amiable, with a touch of melancholy. His muscle-bound legs loosened at the joints and became serviceable for a jig. At this stage alcohol increased his desires towards women, to the constant annoyance of his jealous companion. A little more drink and still deeper instincts were revived. Before killing he was wont to drink himself into this last stage of activity. Hare was able to stand less than his male associate; in drink his natural extravagance increased. Strange, unheard-of ideas rushed into his head in a babbling swarm, that his tongue was hardly quick enough to explain. He would burst into an extempore song, he would rush to a seat and explain the beginning of a marvellous plan to get rich, then, forgetting the end, he would jump among the dancers, and grimace and roar. Later with a little more than he could carry he would become suddenly lumpish and dangerous. The women-kind arrived quickly at the effects usual to their sex: deadening of will, removal of the sense of consequences and fear. Then Mag's nasty temper would begin to rise, and Nell would sing in her corner.

Log's Lodgings in Tanner's Close, where Hare was now landlord of seven beds, as consort of the widowed Maggie, suited the Burke couple. It was at the base of one of those precipitous tenements that keep Edinburgh streets perpetually in shadow. We have the evidence of Mansie Wauch as to how life in them appeared to a honest man:

There was no rest for soul or body by night or day, with police-officers crying, "One o'clock, an' a frosty morning," knocking Eirishmen's teeth down their throats with their battons, hauling limmers by the lug and horn into the lock-up house, or over-by to the Bridewell, where they were set to beat hemp for a small wage, and got their heads shaved; with carters bawling, "Ye yo, yellow sand, yellow sand," with mouths as wide as a barn door and voices that made the drums of your ears dirl, and ring again like mad; with fishwives from Newhaven, Cockenzie, and Fisherrow, skirling, "Roug-a-rug, worst-ling herring," as if everyone was trying to drown out her neighbour, till the very landladies, at the top of the seventeen storey houses, could hear, if they liked to be fashed and might come down at their leisure to buy them at three for a penny; men from Barnton, and there-away on the Queensferry Road, halloing, "Sour douk, sour douk"; tinklers skirmishing the edges of brown plates they were trying to make the old wives buy—and what not. To me, a countryman, it was a real hell on earth.

Among the street-orchestra that terrified poor Mansie in his loneliness was certainly, now and again, the hoarse shout of Nell Burke, with her barrow of shoes to mend, trying to bring the highest attic-dweller, student from Dalkeith, or consumptive Highland sempstress, to put their heads out through the string of washing and mark her in the dizzy gutter below. Night and morning she would trundle and call, while her mate sat and hammered in a back room of Log's, in the artificial twilight, there occu-pied with the fascinating construction and furnishing of a Cosmos, in the centre of which sat like a Buddha a crab-shaped little Irishman, hairy and muscular, meditat-ing impassively the mystery of lesser beings who whirled in a circle past him in his thoughts, like dust in an orbit round the sun. Street lodgers, city, state had sunk in his mind, filled with the obsession of his own needs and plans, to a phantom of the lightest irreality. While Nell went out with the barrow, the Burke universe was in evolution.

Tanner's Close was one of those narrow passages that trail, like ant-runs, from the north side of West Port. The place to which Burke had come home for the completion of his destiny was a basement. In Scottish technical language it was a self-contained flat of three apartments; in English, it had three rooms. The first and largest room, whose top-panes just peered above the level of the gutter, was crowded with beds, frameworks of unbarked pine-stumps, on which were laid grey sheets and earth-coloured blankets. These were at the service of any lodgers poor enough to need them. From this dormitory opened another furnished in the same manner. Farther inside was the cabinet of our cobbler, the reserved corner where the first of his crimes was committed. It was lit by a cob-web curtained window, overlooking a pigsty as far as a blank wall of the next 'land.' Sounds from the non-Burke periphery of the universe reached him muffled by the intervening rooms; from his room it was impossible for any sound to reach the street. Burke thus enjoyed a privacy possibly unique in his life, for that is a luxury as rare for a labourer from mother's bed to common grave as any other privilege. In the inner room, in front of his makeshift last, the bench littered with geometrical cuttings of leather, the slouching box of nails, his hammer, the pungent messes of wax, tar, twine, blacking, his dusty reserves of cob-nails and tacks, Burke passed, like a novice in a cell, through his last period of free-will. Hitherto the

events of his existence, though doubtless governed by in-
discernible tides, had been apparently as indeterminate as
the course of leaves in the corner of the wind. But in every
life, by whatever zigzag it is come to, there is a collecting
place from which the traveller is sent on henceforth in a
line as rigid, as unavoidable, as the deduction from a
Euclidean theorem. The back room at Log's was in
Burke's life such a place, the entrance of a pipe into which
once sucked in he was whirled inevitably on his fate and
deeds, without any possible deviation.

On the 29th November, 1827, Hare rushed into this
back room and announced the death of old Donald. This
Donald was a Highlander, an army pensioner who had
been ailing for weeks in one of the beds in the middle
room. When in health he had been a good payer, and
Hare had let him lie, in confidence that as soon as he could
get up he would go to the Castle for his quarterly due and
pay his reckoning, with a trifle besides for the interest.
But here Donald was dead, owing over three pounds. The
loss of the money seemed certain; Hare was half off his
head with rage and despair; talked wildly of throwing
the ——— in the gutter, cursed his own generosity. Then
suddenly, we suppose, without any connexion with his
trend of thought, as was Hare's unexpected way, blurted
out as he might a blasphemy: the Body Snatchers.

It was Hare, then, that first of the two spoke that word.
Not indeed the subject, but the tone in which he said it,
the eyebrow play, the mouth twisting was the bizarre novelty. Wherever death was in the house in all Edinburgh,
and within a cart-journey around, in square or tenement

or farmhouse, intruding on grief or shocking indifference, as inevitably as the coffin, entered in those days the loathsome phrase. But Hare blurted it out like an invocation to the worm and the rat; an unusual tone. For even three feet under the earth level in an Edinburgh tenement, where the two now talked—especially there—they were frightfully afraid of the Body Snatcher. To the rich it was a monstrous obscenity to be guarded against with forethought and precaution, but to the poor it was the first horror of sickness and the last terror of death, that their bodies, from which it is hard even for the educated to separate in thought their own most intimate beings, and to which literal Calvinism attached the hope of resurrection itself, should be in danger of being unburied by ghouls, carted to the dissection table, and cut to pieces by the apprentice doctors.

The history of the first struggles of the science of anatomy in Scotland, in which this body-snatching is a morbid and curious incident, has been written many times with a wealth of detail that its intrinsic importance hardly deserves. Instead of a frightful dilemma, in which humanity stood frozen between the necessity of burking a young science, or committing a social abomination, as they all thought, we can see nowadays nothing more than the stereotyped laziness and neglect of the legislator. The perfectly satisfactory and simple arrangement that now assures the legal supply of the anatomy schools was possible at any time, and needed no genius to think of.

That it needed the thumbs of Burke and Hare to jog them on their duty is a sarcasm that the Scottish ruling

class never understood. The stupidity of starving a science
of the utmost importance and pride to the State of its essential material, thereby obliging it to approvision itself by the
help of a class of low and unseemly thieves, is gross
enough. It had the customary defense of having lasted a
long time. The law of 'one malefactor's body a year' with
which Scottish Anatomy started when it was a superstition,
has been amplified by that of 'foundlings, suicides, and
criminals' in 1694. This was insufficient even for the needs
of the University School, which against all the interests
of science had fallen, during the eighteenth century, into
the hands of a family, and was passed down, like a peer-
age, from father to son; and many examples of the rifling
of graves, by the orthodox students and by base helpers,
occurred during this period. In the beginning of the nineteenth century, rival schools conducted by brilliant investigators like Barclay and Knox set up in competition to the
official school, and both because these rivals were excluded
in whole or part from the insufficient supplies of corpses
which went to the University School, and still more
because their discoveries and methods had aroused a
tremendous interest in medical studies, resulting in a great
increase in the numbers and enthusiasm of students, Body-
snatching became a crime, or a trade, of huge activity. No
grave was now inviolate. The conscience of hired guards
was never to be trusted, for the schools were prosperous
and desperate; no death-bed was free from the fear. A
trade in the second-hand, be it noted, this Body-snatching,
the supreme branch of that commerce into which Burke
had steered his way. But in its normal exercise Body-
snatching is also a speciality, and Burke is barred by

character from all specialities. This one needed courage, training, resources, qualities by nature wanting to this incompetent egotist, now sitting in the back lair at Log's looking at the grimaces of Hare, pricking with the first notion of a plan 'to do himself some good.' He may have had an envy of the gains of the Resurrection Men before; certainly in common with half the population of Scotland, he knew by repute how they tricked the undertaker. So it is not long before he jags his thumb at the grimy light behind him and reminds Hare that there is a tanner's yard at hand. Bodies are riches; but until now, how to get them? Here is Fate that has tossed them a toothsome bone from her table, to cur and wolf, and they know what to do with it. If dead Donald has no friends to pay his debts, excellent, he shall pay them himself.

So Burke and Hare buy from the tanner the regular sack of bark, and when the coffin carpenter has finished and gone, they prise up the case, hoist out the body and frog-march it to the dark room. Then put the bag of bark, the specific gravity exactly of a wasted body, into the shell, and nail that up for pauper burial. When the town-hearse has passed, they send out one of the women for a tea-chest, for by a mysterious ratio, bag of bark: human body: tea chest: convenient coffin.

After dark, they sold 'the thing' for £7 10s. to Doctor Knox, 10 Surgeon's Square, the noted independent professor of anatomy whose address and reputation for paying the best prices for bodies had been found out somehow by Burke. This Knox, who was ruined as a result of the case, was one of those intelligent eccentrics of whom Scotland has the manufacturing secret. In science he was as remarkable as in appearance, a gnarled little fellow, with 'a blind eye like a grape,' with a coffin-shaped forehead; in character, a squirming package of malice, jealousy and pawkiness who did not disdain to eke out his undoubted attainments with all the tricks of an advanced quackery. Knox was as fanatical a self-admirer as Burke; had the murderer met with a like success in his life-cult of himself, his neighbours doubtless would have had to stand the same spectacle of unwearied self-glorification, as Edinburgh Society from that learned Doctor, and complete egotist, Knox. We are indeed in presence, unlike as the social circumstances and the progress of the disease may make them appear, of two phases of the same character, and it is interesting to watch how both Knox and Burke, to make the objective world of their relation to fellow-individuals and society assimilable in the inadjustable centre of their egocentric universe, were obliged to use the same system.

Knox excused to himself all his basenesses 'because it was a matter of science.' To Burke, his mean swindlings, the agonies of his victims, were only tolerable if he clung to it—'this is a matter of business.' A wavering of the theory even for a second would have brought Burke to his knees, howling for a priest; or sent Knox mad with shame. But till the one stood on the boards of the scaffold, and the other closed a spoilt career 'in the position of show-man to a tribe of Ojibbeway Indians in a circus in London,' it cannot be found that either wavered in his self-hypnotism for a little instant. In later chapters we will come across other souls not less simple or steadfast.

The next step in Burke's unfolding is a phrase, pronounced by one of the students, perhaps by Knox himself as the deal in a second-hand soldier was completed, so inevitable in the progress of his fate that its absence would have had the disagreeable effect of a miracle. Burke was told 'they would be glad to see him again if he had another to dispose of on the same terms.' It was the natural viaticum of a newly-recruited Body Snatcher. Tucking this fruitful word away for future examination, they jogged homeward, the one chuckling, the other drunk before he had had a drop with the feel of the gold in his trousers pocket.

In such a mood the money could not last, and in the little back room, Burke soon had the other gift, the greater gift, the phrase, out of the pocket of his mind. He indeed claims that Hare was earlier curious and hopeful about it. The women certainly heard of it too, and they would have their silly, urgent suggestions that their men should go regularly into the business, hire cart and two spades, and mine cemeteries. But Burke had no cart. An inner logic in him is offended by the form of the suggestion. The more they push him, the thicker rise his objections. All the inhibitions in him are set on edge at the same time, his cowardice, his inertia, his fecklessness. He fears to touch a craft that must have many secrets and a jealous fence of adepts to resent the newcomer. He has a thousand excuses to set against the women's uncomprehension. Violent quarrels break out that scare the neighbours, the three struggling to break through his 'stupidity'; he in a blind exasperation trying to find the word that would convince them that what they propose is 'not in his line,' not in the mathematical line of forces and destinies that is driving him; not into body-snatching, but Murder. They are all at cross purposes.

But now Hare has another trouble on him. Another lodger goes wrong, Joseph, the mumping miller, dying with fever in the middle room. At first Joseph looked as good a shot as old Donald; for there were no friends, nor family. But he was a tedious while about it, and the bill mounted. Then the fever scared other lodgers away. No one would sleep in the same room with him. Joseph was a hard dier. A man who by all natural right owed his body and withheld possession. A sufferer whom it would be kindness to put out of his pain.

But before all could be satisfied, tormented Joseph, angry Hare, greedy Burke, brilliant Doctor Knox, there is a little jump to be taken. Burke is not standing before it in cold hesitation, trying to gather mysterious forces out of the darkness to perform a feat out of natural powers. He is sliding steadily towards this leap with the resultant force of his whole life. There is no moment at which the eye can rest on him in doubt, and see a stationary figure contorted in an effort to conquer his soul and jump. The deed that has to follow has in reality happened long before. Its historical date is the mere intersection of all the momenta that his destiny has stored in him. Burke's course at this deep place is as the projectile that passes in air over a gulf, without the shadow of a check. As the dirty business they proposed to him appears to be full of difficulties and impossible, so the killing of the miller appears to him trifling, easy, obvious. The act for which he is to be punished, the act for which alone society is horribly interested in him, is in his own consciousness an inch in a length of ribbon, indistinguishable and inseparable from the rest except by shears.

So, when they have supped (because the few lodgers are abroad drinking), from his bed (because he is alone) Burke takes the pillow (because it is at hand) and places it over the nostrils of the man (so as not to spoil the body), and when the dying Joseph kicks, Hare (because it might make a noise) seizes his legs. And so they hold, until all is limp (because they know he is dead). Turn for a moment, now, to Hare. His whole life is a bead-roll of incidents held together only by a thread. This night is the latest of his miscellany of fights, brawls, sudden feats: seemingly accidental. He has taken it to his jackdaw hoard of memories with wonder and scrutiny. He will remember every detail of it later in his confession. But Burke, on the contrary, afterward, will have a vague doubt about it. He will fix it awry in the sequence. Did I or did I not, one night in the beginning of my swift straight course pass over a gulf far below? Burke does not remember. Downwards on to scenery of his villainies, at the present speed of his fate he may not turn his head. But Hare is only a passenger on the vessel of Burke's destiny, an accessory that lends a hand when he is told, that may shout a suggestion in the driver's ear. His mood is the meaningless exhilaration of being irresponsibly whirled on forces he could never himself collect. Such is the accomplice, who is neither a rare nor a common component of great crimes, the negative molecule in the destructive atom of Burke and Hare. Two equal fates cannot combine in any great undertaking; therefore there can never be equal responsibilities. Without his Hare, Burke would find another leg-holder, or change his method. Without Burke, a Hare will shoot and skid on his erratic course, making a dog's day of his life, without connection or perseverance, may even continue killing for a time by impetus, but remain in nature a jumping squib, not a bullet.

Now the women-kind, like two delicate ladies who cannot bear to hear poultry killed, come back out of the corridor where they have been holding hands over ears, almost determined to ask no questions. Yes, the poor fellow is dead. The elusive blight of life that kept a good body unsaleable, was it squeezed out or petered out? About this they must not be curious. They may get the kitchen ready for the carousal promised; and one may go for the tea-chest.

Already all details are hardening. The Law of Repetition which dogs the mass-murderer's acts, as the rigor mortis their material is shaping itself. This Law is their unvarying symptom, it is this that forces the plural assassin to act a perpetual series of replicas of his first successful crime and causes the tea-box of Burke, baths of Smith, the Gambais elopements of Landru, the bucket of Haarmann. Even the accidents never vary, once the crime-type is discovered. It is as if their self-made fate, in fully obeyed course, is condemned to a law of monotony, in which not only its own impetus conserves it, but the working of the two factors, lack of imagination, and the hypertrophied instinct of self-preservation characteristic of all such characters. The mass-murderer repeats himself, blindly, because he has no imagination. If he had imagination it would breed sympathy and pity. The complete lack of these feelings is necessary before a man can kill.

He repeats the details of his first crime, because he is afraid the least innovation would endanger a recurrence of his immunity. He has ventured into a morass, full of uncharted pools, and in all further visits he will follow meticulously the prints of his own boots.

But Burke is not yet arrived at the full model of his crimes. The death of Joseph (sold for £10 to Knox) was in one essential particular, unique. If the couple must wait until another sick lodger without friends and family comes of free will to their net, there could not be much more business. As, after the second payment from the doctors, they are perfectly determined to make murder their steady trade, they are forced to arrange for a supply of victims: to go hunting for them. With this, not change but addition, their method is complete. It is Hare, whose eccentricity can arouse trusting laughter as well as fear, to whom it falls to go after the game, in the rank jungle of the Edinburgh streets.

The first quarry obtained is the Old Woman from Gilmerton, one Abigail Simpson, who was burked in February 1828. 'She used to sell salt and camstone. She was decoyed in by Hare and his wife on the afternoon of the 11th February, and he gave her some whiskey to drink. She had one shilling and sixpence and a can of kitchenfee. Hare's wife gave her one shilling and sixpence for it; she drank it all with them. She then said she had a daughter. Hare said that he was a single man and would marry her. They then proposed to her to stay all night, which she did, as she was so drunk she could not go home, and in the morning was vomiting. They then gave her some porter and whiskey and made her so drunk that she fell asleep on the bed. Then (this is part of Burke's statement or confession to the Edinburgh *Courant* newspaper; it is certain he reversed the rôles at this point) Hare laid hold of her mouth and nose, and prevented her from breathing. Burke held her hands and feet till she was dead. She made very little resistance, and when it was convenient they carried her to Doctor Knox's dissecting-rooms in Surgeon's Square, and got £10 for her. She had on a drab mantle, a white-grounded cotton shawl and small blue spots on it. Hare took all her clothes and went out with them; said he was going to put them into the canal. She was a pensioner of Sir John Hay.'

The company had so far progressed by now that the dividends were all as settled as the trade secrets. In the accountancy each sum come by from the doctors was divided sometimes on the spot, sometimes in the square outside, more often in the little dark room at the back, in the ancient Burglar's Sum of $2x + y$, where x is a man's share, y a variable tribute to Mrs. Hare, whose capital rights as proprietor of the killing-shed were always respected. It appears that for some reason, 'either the vigilance of the grave-guards, increase of students or otherwise,' the price of Burke's goods tended to rise. For Mary Haldane, for example, a faded prostitute, was paid more than £10. In some cases, without any special reason being given besides the usual compliment on the 'freshness' of the bodies, Knox, his porter Paterson or any one of his seven assistants, paid £12 or £14 for the subject. The money was quickly spent, partly on carousal, partly on new clothing for the men, finery for the women. Hare, the decoy, insisted on a new coat. The women, from having been 'ragged tanterwallops,' began to be dressed flashily, with new bonnets, fine prints and shawls. But these plain changes in their fortune awakened no public suspicion, which latter indeed, as every case examined will demonstrate, is an entirely overvalued weapon again the rashest murderer, acting, one suspects, only to the hurt of the honest and if anything to the advantage of the knave: a knowing name for corporate stupidity. At first the twain used some craft in the choice of victims, picking out not only those that were ripest, from their bodily weakness and habits of drink, but rather those whose sudden vanishing would wake least comment. But with experience the two became utterly careless of this condition, plucked right and left in the endlessly peopled crowd-streams that passed Tanner's Court, as fancy or chance led them. On the 9th of April 1828 is placed the murder of Mary Patterson, the first of the three cases on which Burke was charged and condemned. Two young street-walkers, Janet Brown and Mary Patterson, both good-looking, and the latter the possessor of a flawless body that was famous in the whole night world of Edinburgh, were accosted by Burke in a grogshop in the early morning, where they had landed after a night in the watch-house. They had not eaten for twenty-four hours, and a gill of whiskey had already bemused the beauty. Burke finding confidence in the obvious signs of this on her face, sidled up suddenly and 'just to see,' began to trespass on Hare's fixed rôle of seducer. Janet, who had a strong head, answered his fawning greeting coldly. But Mary accepted his offer of another drink. He disregarded Janet's refusal and called for three gills of rum and bitters; and himself unloosened by the early potion

and the novel excitement of the chase, he began to talk
with a rush, too fluently, too confidentially, too politely,
after the manner of his kind. Janet's mistrust grew, but she
sat moodily while Mary, who had got to the giggling
stage, found her oily Irishman very amusing. Finally he
dared to invite them home. Janet shook her head, but
Burke in a torrent of lies and blandishments, uttered with
such earnestness that it seemed serious to resist it, swept
away the objections, and they set out together. Quick
reflection showed Burke that it would be impossible to
draw them so far as his own home; he decided to take
them to the lodging of a brother of his, Constantine Burke,
who was a scavenger in the service of the City Police, in
Gibb's Close, Canongate, just at hand. The interior of
Constantine's lodgings clashed with the claims Burke had
been babbling of his riches and station, but Mary was past
noticing and Janet already too fuddled to exercise her will.
More drink was brought. Constantine went to work. Mary
fell across the table and slept. Burke seeing that Janet still
resisted the liquor, and the bottle being empty, urged her
out of doors, and then easily warding her fluttering attempts to get away, took her to a public house where he
plied her with pies and porter. The money in his purse was
giving out. Still the girl kept her feet. They then returned in
the same outward state as they had gone out to the house in
Gibb's Close. Mary was still asleep; but Burke was at his
wits' end with excitement. While he racked his brains to
know how he should succeed in a deed so tantalizingly
near completion, in walks Helen M'Dougal, in a fury,
with Constantine's wife. She sees Burke with his arm round
the sprawling beauty, and blurts out in a fury of jealousy.

Burke starts up, nerves on end, and screeches a command for silence; that not gagging her, he smashes a glass on her head which makes the blood flow. Constantine's wife at this claps on her shawl and goes to find Hare. Janet, whom the incident had frightened, explained herself with finicky dignity and also left, promising Burke, who had turned to her with redoubled squirmings, that she would return. Then Burke, with a solemnity that cowed her, took Helen M'Dougal by the hand and flung her into the passage, locking the door against her in silence. On this Hare arrived, troubled the silence of the room for a moment, then shared it. Three times later in the day Janet returned to look for her friend. Three times, like a child playing round the lip of a pit, she escaped without noticing it. For weeks after she searched their familiar places for a sign of Mary Patterson. In Surgeon's Square they could have given her news. The body was in fact recognized by one of the students; Knox was proud of it and called in an artist to enjoy and record the beauties of his latest subject, who still clutched, as if in picturesque moral lesson, two copper coins in one of her hands. A nameless Englishman, ill with jaundice, two other stray women (one of them Burke claims in his confession, decoyed by Mrs. Hare and killed by her husband alone) were prepared in quick succession, by stifling in the back room 'with an iron bolt in the wall,' for the studies of the Knox school.

In these successful deeds Burke and Hare came to a pitch of confidence and ferocity such that they dared to put irony in their killing. The daughter of Mary Haldane, a prostitute like her mother, whom they had killed and a little 'kenspeckle' or touched, meeting Hare one day in the prosperous rig for which her mother's corpse had paid, was invited by him, with that fawning good nature which the exercise of his trade had settled on him, to come to Log's and hear news of her mother. There she was prepared, trussed and slaughtered, and so kept faith with.

We may seek in vain in any of the documents or evidence preserved for any precise knowledge of the increase in either Burke or Hare of the appetite for killing, the gravest mystery of the systematic murder. For a sight of that we shall have later to look elsewhere than in the dried and pressed records of the Burke Trial. But the unmistakable smell of it seemed to emanate from their actions. Hare's horrific joviality, as if his nerves had fed to repletion, was a phenomenon on which his neighbours remarked; a satisfaction by far unaccountable when the effect is reckoned only of sudden money-winnings, more usually cause of the opposite. He had become a monster of good-humour. The long blood orgies changed Burke differently. Sometimes he would sit for hours in lachrymose solitude, his face streaming with sweat. Then in increasing degree his ferocity grew. Unstable fits took him, when he would intrude on Hare's rôle, and contorting his face in mimicry of his partner's smile, roam the streets for hours, like a tiger uncaged. In one of these prowls he came across an aged beggar-woman and her grandson. According to Leighton's story, he was engaged with an old drunkard, and had already chosen him, eyed his muscles, his throat, and proposed at that very moment to take him back to the den; when the old Irishwoman, catching his accent, came up and asked alms. Burke immediately lets the old man drop, and occupies himself with the unfortunate

couple. Unfortunate indeed, even without this meeting
with the stooping gentleman in the new clothes, for both
were destitute and the boy a dumb-mute. Back Burke
comes as fast as he can lead them to the lodging-house.
That night he throttled the granddam; the next morning
he broke the boy's back, across his knee. Are there grades
in murder? This act is said to have been his cruelest. For
the moment, to the murderers, it only appeared the rashest.
On the top of the slowly slacking fire that the double act
had re-lit and re-satisfied in them both, entered for the first
time an insufferable uneasiness. Burke will have us believe
that the boy's dying look had pricked him; a small neck-
preserving joke in the taste of the times. Among the innumerable fears that had swarmed, concede the eyes of the
innocent boy may have awakened, by mental association,
those of religion. But the principal fear was: what will the
doctors say to this glut of double the explainable quantity?
How shall we convey this double cargo without arousing
suspicion? On the natural rebound, they decided to risk it.
Surmounting the strong distaste that Burke, at any rate,
felt to changing fundamental details in the routine, they
stuffed both bodies in a herring barrel, for the tea-chest
was too narrow. Hare bethought him of an old horse on
whom he had some rights, which had served him in his
pettifogging days. He went to fetch it and the skeleton of
a cart from the keeping of a friend. These changes in
method had put Burke in a shivering humour, and they
set out at nightfall, haunted men. When they reached the
market-place, at the entry of the crowded Grassmarket,
the horse stopped dead, as if a hand had seized his bridle.
They could not get him to budge, by either whip, fist,

or oaths. Burke afterward said: 'they thought the old horse
had risen up in judgment against them.' From this terror
Hare pulled them, by the desperate device of calling a
porter, who, by equal marvel, consented to carry the barrel on his hurley without questions to Surgeon's Square.
Hare, whom the moment of supernatural peril seemed to
have roused rather than abashed, hoisted the barrel into
the dissecting-room unaided. They were paid £16 for
their produce. The bodies were so stiff that all had to lend
a hand to haul them out of the barrel. A blind, joyous rage
seized on Burke and Hare when the act was completed.
They returned to the spot where they had left the horse in
charge of a beggar, led it, now unresisting, to a tannery
near by, and Burke cut its throat. Then they discovered on
the body of the horse, with an hilarity they could now
afford, traces of the hand of kindred spirits. The knackers
pointed out that many old sores on its back had been cun-
ningly filled with tallow and pieces of pared skin from
another animal stretched over them.

The reaction from this incident on Burke was a depres-
sion, to cure which he went, with Helen M'Dougal, to
Falkirk to visit some of her relations. Hare, on the other
hand, was swollen by the dominating part he had played
in the danger, and communicated the mood to his wife,
who is said by Burke at this time to have proposed to sup-
press and sell Helen M'Dougal, 'as she being a Scotswom-
an, they could not trust her.' Burke's holiday therefore may
have been in part an ignominious flight, to save his partner
by distance, where will lacked. It restored his nerves. He
came back with new projects, and when he found that
in his absence Hare, still in masterful humour, had dared

to kill for himself—a rag-picker or basket-woman—sell her body for £8 and keep the money entirely for himself, there was a wicked quarrel: after which Burke and his mate removed from the bloodthirsty little cabinet at Log's to lodge with one John Broggan, a carter, who was Nell M'Dougal's cousin. This was not far; it was a one-roomed apartment abutting on waste ground behind the West Port. Burke furnished it with a bed-box, two stools, a pot, and a chair.

Here Burke straightway commenced with one of the plans he had made on holiday. At Falkirk, he had invited a girl—cousin of Helen, Ann M'Dougal—to visit them in Edinburgh. She came in due time. Burke, either because he was still shaking over the affair of the dumb boy, more probably because by flattery he wished to bring Hare into partnership again, trusting later by mere contact to recover leadership over him, pretended that aid of his partner was indispensable. Hare arrived, with the hands that were his only tools, and Ann was profitably sold from Broggan's house. This Broggan received thirty shillings, possibly symbolically, to quit his lodging and the town. A red haze now settles on their doings, which it was impossible even for them to disperse. Henceforth, the chronology, even the numbers of the dead, is forever unknown: until we come to Daft Jamie and Widow Docherty or Campbell, for whose murders only, with that of Mary Patterson, Burke was afterward indicted.

So then, as if concerned with an allegory, Burke and Hare, miserable humanity in quest of a living, have butchered Beauty in the person of Mary Patterson, Infancy in that defenseless dumb boy, as well as a flock of

creatures in like condition to themselves. Now they turn
their undaunted thumbs against Innocence, for which this
Daft Jamie can easily stand. He was one of those inoffensive imbeciles for which by ancient and virtuous tradition
the Scottish race still keeps a respectful affection. His
killing was regarded by the whole nation as the height of
the guilt of these men, as that of the old granny and her
boy was in a sense the lowest deed they had practised, as
if there was some supernatural wickedness attached to it,
like a blasphemy. Jamie was a known character in the
Edinburgh streets, before the discovery of his murder
made him famous over the whole land. He had that abil-
ity, so often found in his similars, of answering in double
sense, with a hidden and unconscious aptness that surprised like the sudden wit of real children, and smacked
of prophecy. All his idiosyncrasies but one were admirable; all were pardonable. He was scrupulously clean, peaceable, though very strong, affectionate to the whole world,
even to the tormenting boys. His only fault was a liking
for drink. On this the accursed couple played to entice
him to Burke's lodging at Broggan's, and there after a
horrible struggle they took possession of his body. In this
killing, Burke received a terrible bite on the hand, which
in the legend grew into a cancer that without the rope
would have carried him off in the end: a detail which
Emile Zola may have come across and copied in his
Thérèse Raquin. In this case the pair reach a height of
rabid audacity that is extraordinary; for the boy was a
figure, almost a public character, and both the recognition
of the body and a general search into his fate were almost
inevitable. The first came about and, though at the trial

the subject was barred, it appears certain that Knox pushed his pitiful inconscience to the limit of its possibility. He denied the resemblance which his students recognized, but gave instructions to use the body out of its usual order in time so that it could be got out of the way. Still more unaccidentally, the head and the foot, which was a notorious malformation in Daft Jamie, were first removed.

Again that fool, public suspicion, had no bark. In later years it was said that a rumour, something unformed and intangible, spread at this stage through the city, that horrors unknown were abroad, that a tremendous crime against or by whom no one knew was on the point of discovery. Such corporate premonitions are by no means unknown, but the evidence for this one is quite impure. It was of no utility, in any case. Burke and Hare safely reached the last stage of their course, where arrive all mass-murderers if left safe long enough, in which the criminal as if ripe on his branch comes to a natural termination of his series, and plashes to the ground with his own weight. In this phase, the immunity and the intolerably blown-up greed for killing has given them a dizziness that if they were not stopped would have driven them with their weapons into public places to run amuck on the crowd. Their time is up; we will see this hanging season re-enacted in the lives of other villains. No longer content to hide in the shadow of back rooms, they brought out their snares in public at full midday and shook them in the faces of the victims. The case of the brisk little woman belongs to this last phase. Burke picked her up. He claimed relationship because she was named Docherty, and brought her home. Two lodgers, honest beggars

named Gray, were thereupon asked to leave the room,
with as many open nods and winks as if the mad murderers had come to think that they and the whole world
were accomplice in their deeds. Gray and his wife went
obediently to spend the night at Hare's now almost
deserted lodging house. When they returned next morning,
though quite without any aim to their suspicions, they
were in a state of irritated curiosity. First, they ask what
has become of that queer little Mrs. Docherty. Helen, who
has the black dog squatting heavier on her shoulders than
usual, rasps out a curse, a charge and an explanation.
She is outside the major frenzy of confidence that has
seized on the more guilty trio. Mrs. Gray settles herself
near the bedfoot; Burke gives her another wildly knowing
nod; seeing she looks at him blankly, he snaps at her:
'Keep out there, out of that straw.' Hare and his woman
depart, not noticing this cross-play; Burke follows, grumbling. Mrs. Gray, when they are all gone, with the frightened eagerness of Bluebeard's last wife, sneaks to the
forbidden spot, scratches the hay aside, sees the body of
brisk Mrs. Docherty, naked, cold, blood-spotted. She
screeches to her husband; both desperately pack their kit,
and are only through the door when Helen M'Dougal, the
colour of the corpse, pushes into them on her belated
return. Mrs. Gray can do nothing but stare at her; Gray,
called to explain this trembling flight, strokes his chin and
in a very cautious undertone says: 'They have seen *her*.'
Helen, as if she were suffocating, then lumps on her knees
in their way and begins to pray to them; it will be worth
their while to keep quiet, even to £10 a week. But the
Grays cannot be stopped; they edge past her softly, with-

out any further reproach, for they are afraid of her. Outside they take to their heels, their knapsacks thumping on their backs, to the police-office. Naturally in the invigorating air of the witness-box of a great trial they afterwards found a finer version of their words; to us, their action in refusing Helen's money, though completely penniless, could stand alone. Later, that warm-hearted Edinburgh public that 'the tale stirred to its marrow' raised a subscription for the Grays, the only honest people Burke and Hare came across during the pursuit of their business. It reached a total of nearly £10 when the newspapers closed it. Meanwhile Burke, Hare, and Meg, who had returned, hardly listened to Helen's panting story. They are all blind or insane. What, run and hide now? When Knox and the most powerful gentlemen of Edinburgh are their clients, when only last week the doctor's gatekeeper had hinted at a bigger scheme, a wholesale scheme, to be worked from Glasgow, even from Ireland? To run now, when the world's throat was in their fingers? Hare laughed, Mrs. Hare laughed, even Burke laughed at Helen's idea. To show her still more plainly where their pride had grown, they fetched in a porter, one McCulloch. So far from hugger-muggery, he, a stranger, should do the dirty work, stuff the body in, cut off a wisp of hair that stuck through a chink and carry it on his back in broad daylight to Surgeon's Square.

Now this last insanity is done, still society takes no notice. All Edinburgh is a rabbit warren that still thinks no harm of the weasels at play at the mouth of their holes. Not till eight o'clock that night does a police-officer (Ferguson) arrive at the room where the bed straw is

soaking. He finds them all drunk and singing. Already half
a defender of these merry, mad fellows against the snivelling couple Gray, Ferguson takes Burke's all-embracing
winks and returns them. For form, he asks: 'Where are
all your lodgers?' Burke turns round laughing and says:
'You've got one or two of them with you now.' He is not
even angry with the Grays. So it goes on, stupid question,
waggish reply, until Helen, at the last moment, when the
police-officer is snapping his notebook on which he had
ended with 'case of neighbours' jealousy,' makes such a
reply, in her anxiety, as to undo the life of the others.
Burke had just said, 'The old creature left us at seven
this morning.' Mrs. Burke, at the same question, must
improve it with her lie, 'At seven last night.' As if it was
a necromantic word, as soon as it is uttered the whole
hideous structure, Burke's life, Hare's life, money, blood-
passion, and the whole edifice of murder-fed Scotch science and Knoxism fell in headlong ruins, in one moment.
As if he had indeed faintly heard something fall, Ferguson
is startled, goes to the bed towards which Mrs. Gray has
lifted her justiciary finger, and so finds the rags, the spittle
and the blood.

This is the narrative to which Lords-Justices had now,
by deputation of ancient law, to fit an end, in which must
carefully be dosed public revenge, social utility, and the
glorification of the moral system. It is never a facile art:
with Burke and Hare in 1828, one singularly difficult.
The crowd's simple wish for retaliation on the vermin that
had harried its flanks needed blood to satisfy it, as much
blood as possible. But by the rules, there must first be
proof before Burke, Hare, M'Dougal, Log could be pushed

to the scaffold. That proof could only come from Knox's books, and its nature must defeat all the other ends which Law and Order would satisfy. The only proof would fatally discredit the new aristocracy of learning which was painfully being built up to replace the exterminated anti-Hanoverian feudality. The fumes of the French Revolution still hung in the atmosphere of 1828; they had combined with the smoke of the coming industrial epoch to form a gas of unknown properties. If Knox gives evidence, he must be tried, or torn to pieces. Instead of a healthful, picturesque moral lesson to the mob of the virtue, the beneficence, the strength of the ruling classes, against whose wisdom no roguery could remain hid, against whose vengeance no unauthorized killing remain unrevenged, the trial would turn into a suicidal spectacle of the sloth of the police, the hypocrisy of power, the villainy of the elect. If Knox could only be separated from the class which had accepted him, and built him into itself, the terrific show of his punishment might be a possible audacity. But with him, the executioner must hack at the neck of society itself, with which he was inseparably welded. He would defend himself, like a Samson, and pull down in his struggles the whole temple of Bailies, Doctors, Schools, Legislators, even perhaps, crack the Church and State. Knox's evidence was out of the question; let the mob howl as they will, it is better to face them on the ramparts than in the Tuileries. That evidence must be dispensed with or pried out of the four themselves at whatever cost to the perfection of the trial. Never could judges have felt with such bitterness the deprivation of the old method of torture, of which thinkers, theorists, Knoxes of the past had robbed them. A simple bar of iron and a coke-fire would have brought them out of this detestable perplexity and let them give the raving crowd their complete demands: Burke, Hare, M'Dougal, Margaret Log stumbling in a complete row in gallows procession, to the glory of God and His deputies on earth, Law, Order: the powers that be.

Those four horrors are frightened, but mum. They will no more do tricks to please their captors than newly-caught rats in a trap. The only quality in them that the judges can catch hold of is treachery. One death must be foregone, or all will be spoiled. One death? It seems two, for the couples clutch together in doom as irrationally, provokingly as Mary Patterson held to her pennies. They will split, they are yammering to split, but vertically, not horizontally. The atom will disintegrate only after its own law. Finally justice must choose between Burke and Helen M'Dougal, or Hare and Mrs. Log, there is no other permutation. All seems to go wrong for the avengers in this case. That cleavage is the worst possible. For Burke they must have. He is the leader. Besides, he seems to have scruples, certainly has the worst memory. Hare would perform his informer's contract, with shameful loyalty. With Burke they will have to fear a faithful treachery. At the last moment, in court, he may play his betrayers false and his co-murderer true, and risk the freedom of the whole squad. But with Burke must stay M'Dougal. No jury will take her for the rope, if Log walks free under their noses. If they could only keep Burke and Margaret Log. That is as impossible as Burke and Hare. So with Burke, and with the off-chance of his moaning, frantic woman, our high, level-handed justice must be content.

With so much lost in the cutting, the gem is small. In the Trial, instead of the natural unrolling of a story in which all the subterranean secrets of human nature are printed, we have the embarrassed scuffle of men who are forced with discomfort to have much to conceal. The complicated mental wrestling of experts on points of law, usually one of the adornments of Scottish trials, is half-hearted and double-length. Burke, when the liberty that Hare won was dangling before him, had cooked a rambling confession, which made matters easier. The spectacle of Hare, his clowneries restored to vigour by the joyous surprise of his liberty, shocked the public and put the judges in a glum fury. Instead of the full programme of investigation into the deaths of three victims, only that of the brisk Widow Docherty was discussed. Daft Jamie and Mary Patterson remained only incidentally avenged. The great drama degenerated into that pointless, wearying pow-wow, which is ironically named a 'legal farce.' The condemnation of Burke, the acquittal of his paramour ended it.

The traditional side-show of the condemned cell was now opened. To it flocked the troupe of pastors and priests, neglecting the common rut of souls for this high-seasoned sinner; the string of literary men agog for easy word-painting; the fashionable sketchers in search of a subject that would sell. The newspapers were column-crammed with impressions; parsons who disclosed that their sheep was conscious of his doom, and even more frightened of the second, lingering execution they had revealed to him than of that to which he stood condemned. Literary persons showed their surprise that this mean murderer was short and unhandsome. And fashionable painters, in their immemorial way, related how after he had willingly posed, this penniless cobbler asked them for a sixpence as reward. The great ogre, the mob who could not read, consoled itself for the moment with the only reparation of which it had not been bilked. Burke remained.

His remarks and occupations in the condemned cell have been preserved. They have little to tell us but what we knew before: that a man who has confessed to sixteen murders in the space of nine months, is still a human being. He complained of the cold, of money owing to him by Knox on the last body; of Hare's treachery. He showed great, edifying interest in the various plans urged upon him for making sure of a good living the other side of the grave. On these towards the end he spent hours of close thought. The other consolation of the damned, a sense of being a public figure 'after all,' led him to ask for a decent suit of clothes to make his last appearance.

On the 28th January 1829, justice is ready for the act that is to close in the hole of the West Port murders, and by one last throttling turn it all into a moral story. A squad of municipal workmen put up the cross post and stairs, watched by a vast crowd which mumbled over every nail, every board, to extract the keen foretaste contained. Mighty 'lands' tower sheer over the gallows; their usual population is displaced by hordes of wealthy sightseers, who by more than opera manners, in spite of a rain-storm, are in their windows by break of day. At eight o'clock our poor jackal was brought out for his ordained end, which was accomplished within a quarter of an hour, with all the educative ritual of public execution; the great shout; the muffling; the slight hitch, caused by the nerves of the stage-frightened hangman; the last prayer and signal; the silence, the drop. The undertaker's men give his feet a twirl. Burke, like a big curiously shaped top, spun out into the air and out of life. His body, with platitudinous aptness, was taken for dissection, not to the broken-windowed establishment of his old patron, but to the rival theatre of Doctor Monro, where it was shown to all fashionable Edinburgh, to the great good of the house. His accomplices had a more tedious fate. The unappeasable mob made clumsy attempts to kill them for itself; in the end had to be content with effigy-burnings of Knox, and a hue-and-cry after Hare and the women on their release. One by one they disappear from history. Knox was the slowest to depart; but in a few years of snarling obstination, he, too, had left Edinburgh, the school, all his comforts and honours and set reluctantly on his way into the winding back streets of ruin and decline, where only fable can henceforward trace him.

The
Imperialism
of
J.-B. Troppmann

Troppmann! Qui es tu? d'où viens-tu? pourquoi
es-tu aussi pervers? Dieu t'a-t-il donné une force
morale égale a celle des autres hommes? l'éduca-
tion est-elle venue sur toi, ou as-tu été livré sans
défense à tes sombres entraînements? . . . Homme
ou monstre, Troppmann est une créature de Dieu;
écoutez; on vient de tuer Jean Kinck; Troppmann
sait qui'il n'y a pas de pain dans sa maison.

—*Plaidoirie de Maître Lachaud*

WHATEVER MOVING OUTLINE OF NECESSITY, IMPLYING laws at work, there may be in the career of William Burke, many enigmas remain which the light did not let us thoroughly examine. There is the remarkable *unsympathy*, the exclusively professional point of view: there is the killing-pleasure, or sensuality of hunting; there is the contempt of punishment, which grew to a hypertrophied last stage in Burke. All these stigmata were in Burke as they are in all mass-murderers, but in a simple and rudimentary form, sufficient and no more to perceive their likeness to qualities that many normally ambitious men possess. There was another characteristic, even dimmer: the personal myth, to supply the needs of which the man was ready for any disgusting danger or toil. Burke certainly knew some tale about himself, in which he played the hero's rôle. He was spinning a day-dream universe in which nothing counted but himself, which he sustained and which sustained him until his last choke.

Even this is not a novel phenomenon. Many peaceful citizens are supported in the fatigues of life by a similar secret fantasy which no one but themselves may know. Of Burke's daydream neither do we know the plot in its crude entirety, nor its history of growth, nor the method he used in preserving it against the shock of contradictions of the 'real' world; nor (though we can guess at them) the supporting influences of contact with that other false dreamer Knox, and the prestige of system he represented. For our herborizing, we must now take in hand a better preserved specimen. This, tap-root and leaves, we find in the case of Jean-Baptiste Troppmann. This man was born in the small town of Cernay in Alsace, in the year 1849. He was executed at Paris, the 19th of January 1870, for the butchery of a family of eight persons, so that his short life roughly covers the period of the usurpation of Louis Napoleon over the French; from its timid beginnings in fraud, until its downfall began to throw shadows. The coincidence is not idle. They never met, but there were constant relations between the monster and the Emperor: twenty years of pressure of Bonaparte on Troppmann, then six months revenge of Troppmann on Bonaparte.

Often the trial of a mass-murderer, as if by chemical action of the passions engaged in his life and punishment, performs a sort of distillation of the times in which it occurs, however vaporous and transitory they may be, that gives it a place in history, at any rate in social history. Rarely is this more obvious than with this Troppmann.

His father, Joseph Troppmann, was a mechanic, ingenious as well as industrious, who had invented, among several minor contrivances, a machine for the making of 'busettes' of papier mâché—tubes used in the industry of weaving. It was a practical invention, and for years after the Troppmann case continued in use in small factories in Tourcoing and Roubaix. He had little sense in money matters. These two linked characteristics of the uneducated inventor, ingenuity and business incapacity, were inherited in a certain degree by J.-B. Troppmann. He grew up in a household where want and uncertainty waited at every meal. His father had once been bankrupt. Fear of a second appearance before the courts had soured him before his notorious son was born. The contrast between his lot and that infinitely more peaceable and pleasant of his intellectual inferiors irritated the father's difficulties; Troppmann *père* was always on the verge of belief in a world-conspiracy of persecution, devised by rivals to prevent him from vast fortunes which his inventions deserved. In his unending warfare against bailiffs and creditors, he could only entrench his soul in megalomaniac projects, to which his brain gave enough substance for plausibility, at any rate in the family circle, but which his other shortcomings were as continually destroying. His son, Jean-Baptiste the murderer, was the youngest of a large family. The mother, with intelligence enough to understand the projects of her husband, but not to see the real reasons for their everlasting failure, had been through her married life swung from crises of hope to despair, tossed from dreams of sudden fortune to irksome privations. She was fully infected with the suspicions of her husband against

society and the times. These circumstances acting on her
nature brought her to an inward antagonism, a purblind
misanthropy in which were lumped not only her husband's
creditors, his rivals, both mythical and real, the women-
cousins who were better dressed and fed than herself, but
Joseph Troppmann the father himself, half-comprehended
cause of her unhappiness: his plans, his hopes, and especially 'his' children, that is all except little Jean-Baptiste,
the latest born, to whom she devoted a fierce affection.
The occasional cause of such favouritisms is doubtless
never to be learned by an outsider. There are such secrets
in most marriages. A favouritism may fall upon the eldest
as often as the Benjamin; its value to the mother is obvious as convenient drainage for her sore emotive self, but
hardly ever either to the peace of the family or to the
favoured child himself. This baby, Jean-Baptiste, before
he could talk, became the sole confidant of the badgered
woman; to him alone she showed her tears and made her
complaints. As he grew up the relationship became even
closer and more exclusive—to the frequent rage of the
husband, and the bitterness of the other children. Every
titbit was for the youngest: not usually stolen from the
mouths of the rest, but from the mother's own share, for
she was in her way a conscientious woman; every comfort, every indulgence. He grew up undeniably 'spoilt,'
which showed itself not by peevishness, but by a retired,
convinced egoism, apt to sullenness, inclined to long mal-
ices rather than outbreaks, which latter the ever-watchful
hostility of the father discouraged. Young Troppmann's
heart was educated by his mother. From his father's
thrashings he learnt how to dissemble. At a somewhat

later age than ordinary, he entered the village school and
went on quickly in the elementary studies. At home, he
was always at his books, at a table set for him in the
kitchen, so that he could be at his mother's side. At
school, he walked by himself, living in a spiritual corner,
away from dealings with the other boys, even his
brothers. The secrets and worries that his mother confided
to him as well as her part of his father's angry suspicions
against a world that would not make him rich, Jean-
Baptiste took for himself. He felt always older and more
important than the rest of his school-mates. He had secrets
before he could understand them, worries before he could
write, pride before he could spell. The children of his own
age treated him as if he was already grown-up. Afterwards, when they learnt the force of his malice, the unnatural length of his revenges and his careful perfidies to
satisfy them, they detested him. If Jean-Baptiste had been
weak he would have become the butt of the school.

From this he was not saved by any physical advantage.
He was always small for his age; his mother's pampering
had increased a congenital tendency towards indigestion.
He was a yellow, spidery little boy. But his concentrated,
prematurely determined nature came to the rescue. In his
first fight, before the enemy had made up his mind, Jean-
Baptiste was upon him, and striking in the midst of the
process of words and half-joking sparrings which usually
precede such affairs among youngsters, with as much decision to hurt as a cornered rat, he overwhelmed him. Suc-
cesses such as this gave him a fixed confidence in his power
that made up for his weak muscles; and the exercises that
it led him to undertake, especially jumping and running,

let him correct them. Such was his belief in himself that no
schoolboy feat of agility seemed out of his power, and
each success increased his taste for astonishing the rest.
His infirmity of stomach never left him; but he became a
creature of leather and steel.

At home the influence of Jean-Baptiste's mother increased as he grew up. There was a definite teaching in
her unarranged confidences; perhaps she did not know it.
He did. The strict deduction from these criticisms, complaints, sorrows with which she saturated the boy was: Be
Rich. How? The only method on view in that shiftless
family was: Be Inventive. With this and a fair education,
an unbounded will, a profoundly rooted sense of grievance, Troppmann left school at fourteen, and entered his
father's workshop.

Here was a new world to cow and impress. The workmen, carelessly contemptuous of the father, whose continual money difficulties they well knew, were not inclined
to make easy room for the yellow-faced morose son. His
own elder brother Edmond, full of brotherly grudges,
seemed to abet them. One day, Jean-Baptiste in the midst
of some heavy workshop practical joke against him, which
his brother at his lathe was loudly enjoying, suddenly laid
down his work, seized a hammer and without warning or
a word sidled over and smashed Edmond in the face with
it. The blood flowed. Edmond sobbed out, half fainting:
'You are another Cain.' The word was remembered. On
another occasion, Troppmann impressed his mates. A
workman, some cold morning, slipped on the workshop
floor and his sleeve brushed the spinning axle of the main

power and hooked. At his yell, young Troppmann leapt across a trestle in the way and without making a division between the two actions took the man by the wrist and tore him away, as a panther carries a goat over a hedge of thorns. A feat, mark; not a service. No other speed could have saved the man's arm. Troppmann became more popular; it increased his pride, not his sociability. In slack moments in the workshop, of which there were indeed many, he would vie with the others in feats of address and strength; where there was some knack, or where a boundless confidence and determination could help him, the fellow would win. He had discovered a ready-made jiu-jitsu in his nervous force. Nevertheless, in the workshop he was in a larger world, open to influences larger than his mother's. The spirit of the times is as unavoidable by a growing man, as well as hard to rationalize, as the weather. For one and the other there is a complexity of causes, a multiplicity of effects that resists simplification. The twisted plant of Troppmann's life had, inevitably, been taken out of the overheated stuffy greenhouse of his mother's unhealthy companionship to an open field, on which work winds and rain and sun that cannot be tempered. Wither or bloom, datura-apple or good cabbage, Troppmann had now to suffer the laws of the general weather of his society.

That is the prevailing ideal of the Second Empire. This, for a part, which we have no scale to measure, proceeded from the character of Louis Napoleon himself, and from his career, which was that character in action. We have outlived the fashion for explaining all history by rule

of kings and politicians; the great factor of economics has
fully come into its own; but in any study of social phe-
nomena among men who are imitative as soon as they can
eat, the influence of the Exemplar must assuredly be reckoned with. The actions, tastes, ethics of the Government,
be it despot, clique, or caste have intrinsically an attract-
ing power for each person in the mass of a state, if only
because they are manifested on a platform and at a height.
Newspapers, public gossip foreshow them, as a staple of
interest, very often with approbations and praise that cannot fail to increase their natural attraction. If the reigning
persons are nonentities, their example is never less than an
encouragement for plodding folk. Where their nature is an
anomaly, in conflict with the economic tide of their country, as a spendthrift Court in famine-times, it is true that
it must lose all influence, except on an irreducible minor-
ity in immediate contact, and indeed embitter, advance
and excuse a general revolution, as in the supposed case
of Marie Antoinette. But when the personality of this
Exemplar instead of being dormant, or hostile, meets the
economic factor at the top of its swing, its faculty for
arousing imitation is tremendous.

Louis Napoleon stood in this relation to his subjects.
Himself not free, obliged to foster new riches to secure his
own new power, cut off by his origin from breeding, by
his education from religion, by his crimes from virtue,
he was whirled by his fate into the prow of a state that
was in rapid industrial evolution. The July Monarchy, his
predecessor, in spite of the beginnings of railways, steam,
machinery, left in its flight only a nation of economic
units. The dominant feature of French life before the Sec-

ond Empire was still, on the one hand, the small farm, on the other, the small workshop, which on a majority of occasions meant a peasant-holder, and an 'artisan' working alone, for his own account. It was an intermediate and unstable phase which almost contemporaneously with the *coup d'état* of Louis Bonaparte slipped into the industrial coagulation of modern times. The unexplored resources of the machine were almost suddenly set on the move, in an evolutional avalanche that has not yet stopped. As if feeding on itself, human invention rushed from novelty to novelty, each new idea giving a start to ten others. As each became more powerful and complicated, it drew into its service a larger reservoir of capital, and collected the proletariat of labour out of its isolated work-rooms. France of the 'sixties changed with acceleration into Industrialization. Such a period necessarily offered with one hand, to the possessor of capital, enormous fortunes quickly acquired, to the isolated workmen sudden relief from their crisis of unemployment; with the other it threatened inexorable ruin to the man who had fallen asleep on his investments, and to the small master a no less pitiless extinction. A social upheaval followed necessarily this economic welter. Property, wealth, not only increased with a startling bound, they changed hands daily. While the lot of the workmen hardly changed for the better, the class of bourgeois was greatly increased and the possessions of those who had sunk in the race were shared out by a new class—speculators, industrials, inventors. To the head of this changing nation savagely pushed himself the Bonaparte, the man of December, through blood and perjury.

His advent was thus in perfect timing with the social movement which at the same time he figured and excused. Of
all parvenus, he was the latest come. He was push and
ruthless business in person. By whatever road of jobbery
and daring the new rich of the nation had arrived, Louis
Napoleon outmatched them. On his brand-new throne,
surrounded by his 'knights of industry' he seemed the supreme sanction to the chase for success in which the whole
nation was now engaged; the contrast between his adventurous past and dazzling present was the model and the
romance of a whole generation. The case of Mussolini
offers some faint parallels; but his predecessor, the 'Apache
Prince,' did not deign even these banal wrappings of patriotism without which the Italian never ventures; he offered no other justification for his ambition than the 'will
of the people,' and a guarantee against the power of the
poor. With such necessities in their daily life, and an
Exemplar such that to talk of honesty in his presence
seemed a covert sedition, it is not strange that young men
who had another dream than fortune, and the frenetic
pleasures and honours it would bring under such a rule,
were rare in those times.

No one, in any case no one that young Troppmann
was likely to meet in his family circle, was so inclined.
Troppmann *père* is a manifest of the times. His sick wish
for fortune, his lifelong disappointment which is the measure of his greed, with which he infected first his wife then
his son, were not curious in him but typical of a whole
category of the disappearing artisan. Thousands like him
were seeking to accommodate themselves in their changing

epoch and scratch themselves a good place with their inventive powers alone—fruit of their years of intelligent and independent work in another period. This elder Troppmann was one of that majority that failed. The greatest difference he can claim is that he had a keener view of the prizes, a greater horror of the inevitable penalty of failure than the average. The mother accepted the ambition that ate through her husband's soul, but revealed, openly or unconsciously, to her favourite Jean-Baptiste his father's failure. The rest of the children, without in any way denying the spirit of the times, seem to have resigned themselves to a place with the rest of the new proletariat, and curbed their necks under the wage yoke.

But the youngest Troppmann was not made like them.

Uncertain yet of the exact direction in which he should push his great attack to the conquest of riches and the approbation of his Emperor, he continues to learn. On the one hand chemistry attracted him, rather than his father's mechanics, because its apparatus could be assembled in private, without recourse to the workshop lathes. He wished to avoid any interfering help or knowledge of what he was at. Mechanical invention is usually a social pursuit, consisting essentially in the addition and improvement to machines already existing: no good to our Troppmann, who wished to do everything in secret and alone. He bought, gradually, a dozen flasks, phials and retorts, a few ounces of the salts and acids, and set himself in the privacy of his own room—which he kept locked, except from his mother—to mount the steps of his chosen science. In a few years, working in this way, he had taught himself the elements and began to set himself and solve problems with an ingenuity that later surprised the pundits of chemistry. With a seemingly senseless perversity he made his researches, not on the beaten road of common substances where might be found some honest fortune, but in the fascinating province of poisons. It may have been one of those whims to which the autodidact is always prone, or it may also have been that, already at fifteen years of age, he had abandoned hope of any ordinary fortune. Simultaneously with this hobby, he acquired a passion for romantic reading. Not the usual, omnivorous appetite for all that can promise or affect to explain glorious life just ahead to the growing youth who is neither child nor man. Young Troppmann was single-minded in all that he did. He loved but one person, longed for one thing, sought one plan. He had but one book, and disdained all others. This novel, which had the strange tribute of the entire choice of a Troppmann, was the *Wandering Jew,* of Eugene Sue. Many may remember from their own experience that a boy can put into one book as vast and unreal a content as into his first love; how he can find in it glows, advice, promises, private prophecies which the author never dreamed of, and irrespective of its real style pin on it the cloudy manifestation of his whole inner life. But never was the subjectivity of a first literary love more queerly shown than with Troppmann and his only book. The murky length of this romance had but one purpose in the mind of its author: to teach the moral of the excellence of the honest and humble. Troppmann used it as a grimory, a devil's scriptures to instruct him in a life of crime. For he was certainly already determined imaginatively on such a life. The only question that haunted him as he hung over his phials past midnight could now be: what crime? Fraud? Theft? Robbery? Murder? His family, his mother wrangling querulously in the upper room with his father over the bills of the day, seem to whisper: It doesn't matter—let it be quick. The townsmen, every keeper of a shop, every workman that laughed behind his father's back and capped the local millionaire as he passed, said as plainly as may be: It doesn't matter—let it be great. And the newspapers, recounting with reverent gusto the latest hunt-banquet at Fontainebleau, the Court carnival 'at which appeared the Emperor, costumed as a knight in red and black, and Madame de Castiglione as a gipsy magician,' and *fêtes-champêtre* at Villeneuve-l'Etang, the doings of de Maupas, Persigny, Morny, Saint-Arnaud, counselled him with imperial authority: It doesn't matter. Bide your time, but let it be adventurous and ruthless.

So Troppmann, giving himself minutes of holiday while his phials boil, turns over the leaves of his only book, till he comes to the descriptions of the rich life, to the gloomy and roundabout descriptions of the under-world in great Paris where the law of life is, 'Woe to the Fallen'; and most returned to that episode of Rodin, who, coveting the two hundred and twelve millions of the fortune of the Renneponts, suppresses the whole family. Remember Troppmann's remark years later to the witness Dourson, 'He who reads many novels, and has them in his head, falls asleep. But he who only reads one, has a fixed idea.'

Troppmann continued to progress in his science. He

wasted a year in trying to extract morphia from poppy-
heads; he brags about his success to another young workman, in his peculiar way, sardonically, as they pass a
savage bull in a field: 'I have made a medicine out of
opium so strong that one drop of it would make that fellow there fall down dead on the spot, if I put it on his
tongue.' But the truth is that the technical difficulties were
too much for his home-made laboratory. Another year he
does better, much better, with prussic acid. 'He did not
possess the two vessels necessary; so he used two common
retorts, of which one had the mouth larger than the other,
enabling him to put one inside the other. In the recipient
he put a wet rag to cool it, and he heated the retort used
as distilling vessel with a spirit lamp. I am astonished that
a man ignorant in chemistry could think out such an ingenious, intelligent method' (evidence of Professor Rous-
sin). At last he had what he was seeking: a swift poison
that should leave no trace. But for what purpose? At this
period he would have found it impossible to say. And to
those who observed him, his mother certainly, it seemed no
more than a fancy proper to that romantic age at which a
boy buys a dark lantern or a sword-stick to bring a fancy
of danger into the monotony of his days. The insipid waste
that lies in front of manhood, when the gawky boy is only
on ticket-of-leave from the penal servitude of school, not
yet in reach of freedom, too young to love, to spend, to
enjoy, to achieve, that which we call lovely youth.

But the time has come to give over these toys. The
Firm of Troppmann has lurched again into prosperity:
machines à busette have been ordered in the North, one
even in Paris. Some skilled man must pack with them to

set them up in order, according to terms of contract, and with this rush of work it is easy to give the mother pleasure and set Jean-Baptiste on a journey that will do him good. Young Troppmann, in a hurry, more talkative than they had ever seen him before, commended his bedroom key to his mother, with the dozen blackened retorts and his two illustrated volumes of the *Wandering Jew* bound from the numbers, packed an old bag of his father's, and took train to Paris. To the suburb of Pantin, where the factory is that has bought his father's machine. This factory was the first gaunt industrial settler in a shallow plain of small farmers at the gates of the city. Jean-Baptiste is now nineteen years old. He is on the sill of a life that he has inwardly sworn shall not resemble in its audacity and success any that the townsmen of Cernay know, except that of the Emperor himself. He goes, strengthening himself with passages learnt by heart from his book, a dark, fate-ridden young hero, to conquer the world, a very unsentimental, romantic young man.

In Paris he found what he expected: every road blocked with a frenzied crowd, all on the same hunt as himself. Businesses rising, businesses falling into decay; huge public works—the plans of Baron Haussmann were just ending—a wild world in the pangs of sorting itself out into monstrously rich and abysmally poor. Plenty of work for the many, plenty of chances for the few. Little talk of politics, except among the disappointed, 'the fools.' The mass are obsessed with finding and keeping their feet in the economic swirl. Society with its miraculous mechanism classifies Troppmann at the station and unerringly places him in his appointed pigeon-hole, in a mean lodging near the works. There is no trace of loneliness in him. He is a solitary growth. Now, there is an early period in the life of every villain, as in every saint, in which he must withdraw himself in private, as if for initiation. Such a period Troppmann had now reached; and beyond the bare details: that at Pantin he frequented German workmen of a low class, the last contingent of those come to Paris to work on the housing schemes: that his lodging was in the Rue du Chemin Vert, near the workers' settlement of Quatre Chemins, within view of the scene of his future crimes, we know nothing of his doings or progress. He emerges through this short tunnel, after a passage of months which must have been fixative in his life, at Roubaix. Here, the Paris job completed, he had gone to set up another machine. This expansion in the sale of the Cernay factory was due to a partnership with a certain Kombly, or Combly, into which his father had entered in 1868. Beside a quantity of new orders for machines, the arrangement does not seem to have brought Troppman *père* either the capital lacking, or any real relief from his financial troubles. But young Troppmann, whose self-assurance came with a hard polish from Paris, showed neither concern nor respect for the struggling firm in Roubaix; grown a little freer in his conversation, he often expressed contempt for such pettifogging, and opposed to it a *secret* he himself possessed for making a fortune. Among those to whom he made so free was a certain Jean Kinck. This was a perfect model of all, much or little, that Troppmann *père* had hoped for, worked for, and missed, even down to the detail of being a fellow-Alsatian. Kinck had started level with the harassed inventor. Coming to Roubaix thirty years

before as an artisan, he had married a girl of the region
without dowry. Without a tenth of the elder Troppmann's
brains, with the help only of toil and a business sense, he
had swum in the current, stayed his own master and was
now the possessor, besides six children, of three houses in
Roubaix, a cottage and a waterfall at Buhl in Alsace, and
a small factory for brush-making in Roubaix, the whole
valued at over 100,000 francs. Fellow-countrymen with a
patois are ever clannish. Kinck, on their first introduction,
took young Troppmann home with him and introduced
him to his family. The wife, Hortense Juliette, was of different temperament as well as origin from her husband. As
he was credulous, audacious as well as hard-working, she
was suspicious and timid. But the benefit of these qualities (qualities because they could have served her) was
lost in the new circumstances of the family. While she, an
entirely unlettered woman, would have been an alert
guardian for the interests of her family in the humble
estate in which she was born, as the wife of a moneyed
man she rarely ventured more than vague shakings of the
head, or warnings she could only explain by the interpretation of the Dream-book. She did not like Troppmann;
but she liked none of his countrymen except her husband.
Nor could she explain that this feeling about the yellow
wiry youngster with the weak face and strong profile,
morose and boastful by turns, was more than common
jealousy against a set whose talk in a dialect she could not
understand made her husband home-sick, and set him off
on his everlasting plan to move back to *that* Alsace. With
her at work—they were always at work—were her children. Gustave, aged fifteen, whose ambition was to be

grown-up; Emile, fond of reading, especially books of adventure and romance, aged thirteen, who envied him and
imitated him; Henri, aged ten, who was lazy; Achille, aged
eight, who was serious; Alfred, aged six, the handsomest
of all; Marie, two and a half, who held on her mother's
skirt wherever she walked.

The day Jean Kinck returns with his young friend, and
presents him somewhat apologetically to his wife—there in
the high shed, under the light that is filtered through cob-
webs, standing round the littered lathe, the family is complete at last. For Troppmann is come, who is for ever in-
dissolubly to be linked with the Kincks in the memory of
man: the eight of them down to the last. For he is to be
their murderer.

Henceforward they will be rarely parted. Jean Kinck's
liking for the young man's company grows every day. I do
not know if any less normal motive than friendship moves
him; Claude's Memoirs hint things of which Troppmann's
known indifference to the company of women is the only
support. There were obvious reasons enough for the association. Kinck, in spite of his long sojourn in Roubaix, still
felt the exile. Spiritual inadaptability of the sort is usual
among the half-educated. He was a man expansive and
confident by nature, all the more because of the years of
forced friendlessness while he was making his fortune. But
he needed a compatriot to deliver himself. There was
twenty years between their ages; but Kinck had kept
young and romantic in spirit, so that it sometimes appeared that it was Troppmann who was the more world-
worn. His unconcealable envy of the made-man's fortune

seemed to Kinck part of his reward. Kinck tasted the full measure of his success in this envy of a fellow-countryman. Almost as fascinating was the string of ingenious plans that Troppmann would show the end of at times, which tickled the brushmaker's essential romance, battened down for twenty years in the monotonous specialization of his trade. The two saw each other every day. If they did not sup together at Kinck's home, they would meet in a cabaret for the aperitif. Customers saw them sitting together for hours at a corner table in the shadows, talking in a low voice in their Alsatian jargon.

This friendship Madame Kinck suffered, because of its good effect on her husband. His moods and worries were gone. He became light-hearted and gay, careless of business details that before would have spoilt his appetite. 'Troppmann will make me a millionaire one day,' he said, laughing. The plan to emigrate with the family to Buhl in Alsace to exploit the waterfall, which used to be Madame Kinck's nightmare, was almost forgotten now. When he spoke of it, it was with a laugh at his own past stupidities. There was something bigger in his mind.

On Troppmann this constant proximity with a small fortune—he hardly thought of Kinck as anything else but 100,000 francs since he had heard the sum—worked like a baker's window on a hungry boy. He sniffed for Kinck's coming. He would have been content to stand for hours in front of him without speaking, as if his bony nose was pressed against a pane. But Troppmann did more, what he had never done in his life for anyone. He made himself amiable and interesting; suited his talk to Kinck's mood,

spun for him yarns of life in Paris; sneered at the local
people and their ways; explained his theory of the pre-
eminence of riches with complacent deductions for the
fortunate Kinck, who had never had time before to theo-
rize about his own excellent cleverness in the matter of
that 100,000 francs. When Kinck wished it, Troppmann
would delicately weave for him, with circumspection, never
quite pretending to be serious, so as to lull the sleeping
businessman in his friend, good plans, audacious plans for
more money, and roughly sketch easy roads to the heights
of wealth for a man who had conquered the foothills.
When they parted, Troppmann plunged into deep reflections alone, trying, not to decide, but to confirm himself,
in what he had predetermined to do. At the first meeting,
when he saw the family, the first fortune he had ever seen,
the Book bounded into his mind. With the parallel of the
Rennefont family of the Book, his Book, the *Wandering
Jew,* the Kincks' doom was settled. Not in detail; the details pestered him, they made him savage and as full of
vice as a bad dog. Kinck saw him always amiable, rarely
melancholy. But the rest of Troppmann's acquaintances,
while he was seeking for the slippery details of his plan,
learnt to avoid him as a plague. He took to walking alone,
when Kinck was unable to come. He would stride for
hours, feeling his biceps under his coat, racking his brain.

   On one of these walks he left Roubaix far behind and
stood on the banks of a small canal near the Belgian
frontier. After a while two men came up and started fighting. They drew their knives, and one of them ran away.
Troppmann, hidden by a hedge, watched them fixedly.
They helped his thoughts. The conqueror came: passed.

Not seeing the solitary figure he brushed against him.
Troppmann, his nerves on edge, flew out at him, received
an ugly reply, and in five minutes changed into a mad,
raging animal, flung him into the canal. Troppmann
watched the spot where the brawler had sunk. He did not
see him rise; then he slowly returned home. This was one
of the things he told Kinck, who thought it 'a fine thing
for a young man to know how to look after himself.'

No one can measure the weight of action and balance
it with thought. Is the tree more than the fruit, or the fruit
the importance for which the tree exists? A life that goes
to a goal, horrible or high, is interlocked in all its hours.
You cannot by analysis divide the life of a sensualist into
two parts, separated by the loss of his virginity, nor that
of a man-wolf, Troppmann, by his first kill. Beneath such
a salient act hang countless private thoughts which are its
roots, from which no roughness can pluck it. But though
no one detail of this brutality by the canal is materially
new, when all are agglomerated together, newness, an
unfiltrable abstraction has stolen in, baffling your observation. His crimes before were imagination. This drowning
is Reality. Troppmann leapt, when he seized that first
throat, past an infinitesimal line, for the first time into full
Reality. It happened as imperceptibly but as completely as
a descending point on the rim of a moving wheel changes
direction. Henceforth he is in a new state: a murderer instead of a spoilt boy. All the universe he had built round
himself has to take the new strain, as if it were a ship
launched down the slips. Can it stand Reality? If all
our dreams were seaworthy . . . Troppmann's were of the
most uncommon cement; no joints in his selfishness, no

weak rivets in the armour of his insensibility to pity. So he
has the terrible fate of seeing his dream come true. He
felt himself all over; not a scrap of disgust, not a stain of
remorse; a great soothing pride collects on him, never to
abandon him for long from now until his last hour. His
arm was as strong as he had boasted, his ferocity more
than he had believed. And his theory of the world had
come out of its first testing as unsprung as his nerves and
soul. Kinck admired him for what he had done; another
workman to whom he boasted of the deed in a whisper
looked at him with a most agreeable attention. Troppmann
had confirmed his universe.

From that moment his mind was clear. Without any
more hesitation he began to prepare Kinck for death. A
man-killer hunts with fictions, as an angler with mock
flies. Troppmann had already contrived a decoy-story for
Kinck, but before this baptism of reality by the canal, he
was shy to pull it out. It is curious to examine these mur-
der-fables, the fruit of minds with one idea; they resemble
each other astonishingly, like the stories of confidence-men
whom I reckon close kindred to mass-murderers. It is as
if they are unable to get out of the fixed order of ideals
that boxes their inner life. Troppmann, to dislodge Kinck
from the community that protects him, spins him a yarn
which is obviously nothing but an old, discarded dream
of his own, a plan for coining counterfeit money in a deserted ruin in Alsace that he had marked down in his
solitary rambles, the Château of Herrenfluch. He had
abandoned the idea, lacking the essential machinery; but
he has no difficulty, with his newly-grown confidence, in
making Kinck believe that all is ready for a colossal coup

of millions: presses and dies of miraculous model, now in the hands of friends already installed, but anxious to retire from the business; a secluded work-room; the organization for putting the coins into circulation. One small condition remains: they, the gang, want 5,000 francs for their plant and goodwill.

Kinck in the next week makes ready to travel. He is full of mysterious hints to his friends, mysterious confidences to his wife. There is evidence that she was cognizant of the 'great plan,' none that she objected to it. Without conference with her friends and gossips, her suspicions never had any life in them, and the plan could not be discussed. There is a wide rumour that Kinck has been put in the way of millions by young Troppmann; people are inclined to believe anything strange of the grave sardonic Alsatian, as if he were a sorcerer. At last Kinck sets out. He takes with him two hand-bags (*sacs de nuit*); a small sum of money; two blank cheques drawn on the Caisse Commerciale of Roubaix-Decroix, Vernier, Verley and Company; and a hat-box. Enough for a short voyage. Troppmann went on ahead to prepare the gang for the sale. Kinck, by a roundabout route through Belgium 'to distract suspicion,' not from him but from his assassin (if he but knew it), arrives and is met by Troppmann at the railway station of Bollwiller, near Kinck's natal town of Guebwiller. Troppmann has no visible luggage. In his pocket is a bottle of the prussic acid he had returned to fetch. He is in a cheerful mood, but serious, like a workman on a job he likes and understands. They climb into the omnibus for Soultz. There Kinck left his two bags and the hat-box—all his baggage—at the omnibus office, and asked the time of the last connection at night with Gueb-willer. Evidently he intended to sleep with his relatives there. But before that he had some long business in the region to transact. The two walked over to the cabaret kept by young Madame Laevert and asked for something to eat. She was obliged to send out for sausage and bread. Then the travellers set out in the direction of Cernay, on a road which leads past the ruined château. Troppmann took a bottle of wine with him in the pocket of his riding-coat.

Henceforward the living Kinck was not seen again. The same night (25th August) Troppmann returned home to Cernay. Tired and dusty, he went to bed at once. The next morning his firm air discouraged questions, but he did not go to work. His father noticed with respect that he had a new watch, and 'You seem to have saved money in Paris' said a brother-in-law (Henri Saal). Troppmann had certainly changed in demeanour since his travels. Instead of the furious frown and the wicked silence at any attempt to trespass on his privacy, he returned a slow answer to the questioner. 'I have a business in hand which will surprise the whole world.' The others could draw no more out of him. He was not irritated at their questions, only keeping his counsel with the air of one in possession of a satisfactory mystery. Later he went out, and paid for a drink with a bank-note of one hundred francs. In the afternoon he shut himself in his room, writing letters. One of them was a note to Madame Kinck, with one of the blank cheques on the Caisse Commerciale enclosed, made out for 5,500 francs. He knew that Kinck had left this sum on deposit ready for the payment he expected to make. The signature on the cheque was a close forgery.

The covering letter explained that owing to a slight injury to his hand, Kinck had dictated it to Troppmann. It went on to say that Kinck's affairs were going well; would his wife at once present the cheque for payment and send the money to the Guebwiller post office? She received this command on the 27th August; next day she walked to the bank. After many difficulties she was able to cash the forged cheque and posted the money the same night.

Meanwhile, Troppmann waited at home. He spent much time in his room. One afternoon, without telling anyone but his mother, he hired a cab and drove alone to the village fête of Uffholtz, ten miles away, where he watched the amusements and the crowd without getting down from his seat, as if in practice for a public life. During these days he showed no impatience or uneasiness. Most of the time he was taciturn. But by fits and starts, both to his mother and to others, his brother-in-law, the girl at the cabaret, a workman, he spoke of a machine, an admirable machine that would bring him a fortune.

On the 31st August the time has come to set this machine into motion. He hired another cab and drove to Guebwiller. He had to pass the ruined château. At the post office he had a disappointment common to inventors. Some cog was loose, some piston stiff—the postmaster refused to deliver a sealed package, evidently of importance, addressed to Jean Kinck, without a legal procuration from this person. The personal papers presented in that name by the young man did not seem to him sufficient. Seeing the package was sealed . . . Our inventor went away. A little tinkering he thought would soon remove the hitch.

Two days later this young man returned with the necessary procuration, signed by Jean Kinck, giving full authority to 'his son, Jean Kinck' to collect all letters, sealed
and unsealed, addressed to him at Guebwiller Post Office.
But the hitch is graver than Troppmann had judged.
Instead of a small mechanical fault, the truth is his invention is jammed, inextricably locked in a component part of
a much larger machine, the huge machinery of the French
Administration, made by that other engineer of day
dreams, Napoleon Bonaparte himself. Rust and dust collected in sixty years of use have but made it the heavier to
shift. This procuration is no good, it is not legally registered and authenticated before a notary-public. In vain
Troppmann pulls and shakes at it; the most the postmaster
will do is to pass the irregularity, if Jean Kinck junior will
bring a member of his family (for the father is from
Guebwiller) to identify him. You cannot catch a Troppmann, dull-witted, pettifogging 'leather-cushion' of an
official! Troppmann answers, 'I cannot do that, because
we are on bad terms with this local branch of us.'

Next day the pertinacious young man is back, with the
same request, the same document. This time he has risked
his arm too far; like the imprudent workman he once
saved, he catches his sleeve. A woman in the office comes
up to him and takes him by the sleeve, with the familiar
curiosity of an old peasant: 'No, no, you are no Kinck. I
am Jean's cousin's wife, and though I have not seen him
for years, I am sure he has no son of his own Christian
name.' The postmaster is watching, preparing to throw
the law into gear. With a wrench, not the terrified, hopeless tear-away of a fool, but a deliberate steady tug for

freedom, Troppmann replies coldly: 'My name is Jean
Emile; but in any case I will fetch my father to clear up
matters himself.' The old woman hesitates. She has certainly heard the name Emile, fumbles with her memory
for dates. The postmaster stops; Troppmann, dusting his
sleeve thoughtfully, conscious of every inch of the way, as
if he were crawling on a crag, walks out of the door.
There must be many moments like this in the trade. We
can understand them better than the sudden joys there
must also be in murder; the convulsive terrors when things
go wrong, that stop the heart, but must not be allowed to
affect the speed of speech or walk. Troppmann performs
the feat of getting calmly into the cab, giving his direction,
and waiting while the town is left behind. The wildness of
flight is on him, but he endures motionless till he is
brought into Cernay. Then, still firmly controlled, he says
good-bye to his mother, utters such short excuses as he is
obliged and walks steadily to the railway station for the
Paris train. Fighting with himself in silence as he would
with a babbling victim, he wins before Paris is reached.
For there, without the loss of an hour, he takes train to
Lille, where he rests a night and sends a letter to Madame
Kinck, so conceived:

> My dear family, the time has come to disclose my
> secret. I had commissioned Troppmann to get the letters,
> for I cannot leave Paris myself. Troppmann will explain
> in person better than I could in writing. The whole fam-
> ily must come to Paris for two or three days. That won't
> hurt you, for Troppmann has put half a million francs
> in my way. I absolutely must get them. Gustave, you
> must first go to Guebwiller to collect the money. I send
> you a procuration which you must get the mayor at home

to sign. Get the papers ready before you leave. If you
need money for the journey, go and get it from the bank.
I send you a check for 500 francs. I have given all explanations to Troppmann. He will explain everything to
you. You must do everything he tells you.

JEAN KINCK.

This letter, in which there is hardly a trace of the
horrible shock Troppmann had had the day before, contains between the lines the whole of the second model of
his plan or 'machine.' He delivered it himself to the family
at Roubaix, doing the distance from Lille in a closed
carriage, which he kept waiting outside the door during
his conversation. He explained to them that Kinck's injured hand was no better. Then he went back to Paris.

Here he put up, taking the name of Jean Kinck, at
the Railway Hotel at the Gare du Nord. The owner of
the hotel afterwards found that he had never liked his
guest's looks. However that may be, he let him a room on
the second floor. Troppmann spent his time of waiting
outside, only returning to the hotel to collect letters from
Roubaix, and sleep. He ate at his old pension, Rue de
Chemin Vert at Pantin, and made a friend there, a lad
named Jules Aron, mechanics' adjuster, with whom he visited one day the fête at St. Cloud. Troppmann professed
to this boy a passion for dancing; but from when they
arrived to the moment they left, Troppmann sat at a table,
watching his Aron and the crowd amuse themselves, without trying to join them. On another night, at a ball at
Pantin the same thing occurred. Aron thought his Alsatian
friend a stiff fellow, too awkward to please the girls; *we*
can observe another failure of the dream—the passion for

a gay life, his ruling motive, was nothing but a delusion born out of his book. At Uffholtz, St. Cloud, Pantin, he can only sit and stare.

On his arrival he had sent another letter to Roubaix again in the name of Kinck, again hinting at prosperous fortune and inviting the family to Paris. On the 5th of September, Gustave Kinck went to Guebwiller without waiting for the procuration, which his mother had difficulty in obtaining from the Mayor. Gustave put up with his aunt, Madame Roller, whom he found deeply offended at his father's carelessness in not having called to see her on his trip to the neighbourhood, as he had promised. Gustave made that right. He too was a boy fed on romance, who could be more trusted with a mystery than with a bag of sweets; he had the young illusion that most adventures are good. This trip to Alsace, to be followed by another to Paris, a little intoxicated him. But he kept (if he knew them) any details of his father's movements to himself, and every day, full of importance, went to meet the postman to ask if that sealed letter from Roubaix had come yet.

But another wheel in Troppmann's machine had stuck. Madame Kinck, in her haste to carry out instructions and worried out of her life by the delay at the Town Hall, finally received the procuration a few hours after Gustave's departure. She sent it on to Guebwiller, addressed to the Poste Restante. But an hour later, when she wrote to Gustave, she somehow got it into her head that she had addressed the all-important document to him directly at Madame Roller's home, and in the confusion that followed, never abandoned this mistake. Months afterwards,

a detective found the procuration, the dusty, soiled enve-
lope addressed nearly illegibly by a neighbour to Madame
Kinck—she herself could not write—in one of the back
pigeon-holes of the Poste Restante desk at Guebwiller.
Troppmann had cut the interlocking wheels too fine, too
millimetre fine for their material, planning that his victims
would go to their spoilation with the undeviating accuracy
that he himself put into their ruin. Another cog had stuck:
so far in the back that he could never find it out and
replace it.

    Gustave, tiring of inaction, writes letter after letter to
his mother, but being afraid his father would scold for
his disobedience in starting without the document, does
not mention it in his letters to the Hôtel du Chemin de
Fer du Nord at Paris, until days have passed. Gustave
received a letter, still dictated, 'When you have the money
come here at once, by the quarter to ten train from Mul-
house. I will be at the station. Wire before starting. Hôtel
du Nord.' He wires back that he cannot get the money;
Troppmann, standing at his levers, countermands the order
for the Kinck family to come to Paris; there is a shower
of crossing letters, orders and counter-orders: a noisy
grinding of the disordered machine. Madame Kinck, more
and more nervous and unable to remember her slip, writes
again and again to 'Jean Kinck, Paris'; each time comes
a perfectly cool reply, assuring her that all is well, that his
hand will soon be healed enough to write himself telling
her to send another procuration, and get ready to come
'and see for herself how marvellously his business is going.'

    Fifteen days of this, and the situation is out of hand.

Gustave, suddenly feeling a very small boy again, has had enough. He wires to his father, 'Arriving to-morrow, 5.20 to-morrow morning.' He cannot even remember to take the train his father had insisted on, which would have arrived at night. But naturally he misses the train he had announced, and so by another blunder arrives at night after all, very tearful and very lonely. *His* dream of the great life, at any rate, had dissolved very miserably on its first outing. Troppmann was on the platform. He had been waiting with hunters' patience without a break ever since the morning. They go off together, and Troppmann makes Gustave send a telegram to his mother at once.

> 7th Sept. Just arrived in Paris. You must come. Leave Roubaix Sunday evening at 2 o'clock, 2nd class, bring all papers—Gustave.

Then the couple left, 'as if in a hurry,' to find Jean Kinck the father. It was the 7th of September, 1869.

Now Troppmann's monstrous dream-engine is in full pulse, let it sway and rattle as it will. Jean is dead, the son is dead. The father buried under a heap of stones in an old moat, within earshot of the romantic call of night-owls, under the shadow of legendary oaks and pines, be-tween Bollwiller and Guebwiller. The son, his chest torn in great up-and-down jags of the knife, mangled rather than stabbed, lies under a foot of earth in the dreary plain of Pantin, near the Chemin Vert. Troppmann has no fear, perhaps little hope now, nothing but concentration. With a moment's mind-wandering the tangled mass of the wheels of his Plan will fall back upon him. He does not think like a savage beast, but like a man with an impossible, complicated task to finish, like a conductor of a colossal power in a race with death. His days of lazy posing are over. No more St. Cloud fêtes, no more confidences to Aron. His nerves seem to him concentrated in the tips of his fingers, round his mouth, and along the bridge of his nose. He is not conscious of the rest of his body. As he walks, as he sits and waits for the next horror, he keeps touching, smelling his finger tips, stroking his own lips.

Gustave's telegram was well and truly sent. Madame Kinck, on its receipt, immediately began to pack the bags and assemble the papers she had been told to bring. The birth certificates, title-deeds, marriage act, household leases, private ledger, all that fastened the Family Kinck to the institution of property and the State. She was pregnant; one of the neighbours commiserated with her at having to travel 'in such an unhappy situation.' And little Hortense was just over the fever. But all her uneasiness, in which mingled the continual separation from her husband except by letters she could not read, in the handwriting of a stranger, her self-torments for the matter of the procuration, her half-dead hope of a fortune, her fear of the first long journey she had ever taken in her life, pushed her onward with feverish speed. She could not forget to dress the children in their best clothes; the boys in soldier suits with brass buttons, and military, blue-peaked school-casquettes, the little girl in her Sunday silk.

Madame Kinck was so early at the station that she had time to catch a train that arrived at Paris two full hours before she was expected. Troppmann is using these hours to buy tools. At La Villette, next to the abat-

toirs, he entered an ironmonger's shop at six o'clock. It is
getting dark. He entered so quietly that the shop-girl
(Augustine Tabary) did not notice him, and had a shock
when he spoke. He did not use complete sentences, but
phrases of one or two words, such as 'Spade, pick. Not
that. Too heavy, too light.' Pointing to the handles, he
said: 'More solid.' At eight, just as the shop was closing,
he came back to take away the tools, into which the ironmonger had fitted new shafts. The shop-girl came out to
watch him go: saw him board the omnibus for Pantin, running.

Meanwhile out of his calculations and knowledge, the
survivors of the Kinck family have been for an hour in
Paris. Madame Kinck, carrying Hortense and with her
brood nervously clinging to her skirts, hurries across the
hustling courtyard of the station to the hotel just opposite. She asks for Jean Kinck, for her son and for his
friend Troppmann; with an immensely unfounded relief
hears that Jean Kinck is indeed a guest of the hotel,
though the stupid valet seems not to know the others, and
(without surprise) that this Kinck is out. She had come
too early. She asks permission to leave a package in the
office. Then with her whole troop, returns to the station to
wait on the platform where the later train from Roubaix
would arrive. At 10.45 Troppmann appeared there, yellow and queer, dressed in a long greyish coat. He told her
that Jean was at Pantin, with his son, where he would
take them all in half an hour; these last irritating veils of
inexplicability she hardly noticed, now that the end was
in sight. They pack themselves in a growler, and at 10.50
set out to meet Jean Kinck in the night. It is a windy

night, with clouds and a fitful moon. Madame Kinck very
tired sat facing the horse, Hortense on her knees, her basket at her feet, the two youngest ones on each side of her.
Troppmann sat facing her with the two elder boys. Bardot
the coachman heard the talk of his passengers. Madame
Kinck was silent; Emile and Achille tried to see out of
the window and asked Troppmann 'about the beauties of
Paris.' Occasionally the woman asked the young man
about 'some man'; he replied soothingly. At the Flanders
Gate, the coachman stopped. Troppmann put his head out
of the window and said: "It is farther on, at Quatre
Chemins.' At several points he directed him in the same
manner. At last they came to a deserted spot. Troppmann
knocked on the window to stop. He, Madame Kinck, and
the little girl got down, and this first group set out on the
Chemin Vert. The wind had grown strong and noisy. The
three little boys stayed in the cab, and Bardot left his seat
to talk to them and keep himself warm. They were shy,
but told him they had come a great distance to find their
father. At the end of twenty minutes, twenty-five minutes
at most, Troppmann returned. He stood a little away in
the road and called the boys: "Well, youngsters, we've
decided to stay here.' The coachman was paid off—in the
shadow of the side of the road. He saw them all set off
across the fields, the boys trotting beside their friend, then
he returned to Paris.

   Now the Great Operation is finished, the chemistry
of turning a living family into gold, the mechanics of
substituting a new Jean Kinck, Proprietor, into the frame-
work of society. Troppmann returned to his second-floor

room to sleep, not for that night troubling to examine
the papers or luggage, nor even to count the ready money.
These papers to-morrow will establish him legally as Jean
Kinck. All contradiction has been abolished, and leisurely
he will use them for a passport and a ticket to the
Americas. From there he will realize the Kinck property
and shedding even the memory of Troppmann, begin a
new stage of ambition. He would forget about the field at
Pantin, as an enriched scavenger forgets the dirty work,
as the Emperor himself has forgotten his December mas-
sacres. No one in Roubaix will wonder that the Kinck
mystery finally took them to America; no one in Cernay
will be surprised that Troppmann accompanied them.

Next morning early, Troppmann paid his bill, collected his property that Madame Kinck had left in the
hotel office and took train for Havre. A little earlier still,
at seven o'clock in the morning, a farm labourer named
Langlois, going to his work across the plain of Pantin,
had a disagreeable shock. In a patch of lucerne alongside
his path, he saw a quantity of that substance which even
if one has never seen it before is unmistakable for any
other, whose colour seems perceptible by more than the
eye—fresh blood. He stopped and saw, beyond the field,
where it was ploughed land, smaller pools and spots of
the same tint, like a path. At the end of this run, as if to
mark its end, was the white tip of a handkerchief sticking
out of the soil. The straight furrows hardly wavered over
the spot. But the level of the ground bulged there. Langlois went and scratched with his stick over this ugly un-
evenness. Then dropped stick and bundle and stampeded

back to the road, for he had touched something soft and seen through the brown earth something white and something like hair.

Troppmann's great plan had made short circuit.

The current passing its first conductor discharged in the Police Office. The farmhand, Langlois, although he fell down twice in the road, was quick on his business. The Commissioner himself, with his two gendarmes, in turn was galvanized. They ran back to the field with spades and picks. Another mounted the omnibus at Pantin, to tell the authorities at the Clock-Tower, the Prefecture and Monsieur Claude, Chief of Police, that they had been robbed, cheated, outwitted again. For what else is a great crime, than a great defeat of all the gendarmes, detectives, magistrates, judges, juries and hangmen of a society which pays them, because it hopes one day, somehow, to be rid of criminals? All nations surrender to the will of police the personal liberties of its citizens and their right to protect themselves, not only to ensure revenge, but safety and peace. The horrible power of prisons, courts, hand-chains, whips, bludgeons, ropes and guillotines is given to the police organizations in the ever fallacious hope that these will save families from Troppmann, bodies from Burke, sisters from Landru. Every murder is a proof that the system is for its larger aim incompetent; as every condemnation to death is a plea for another trial for the penal system. In normal times the quickest witted nation, distracted by the pretentious evidence of the detectives, the hounds that are always catching the wolf after he is gorged on sheep, the solemn recapitulations of judges—for ever

nailing up another skin as a warning that never acts—
seldom pierce the deception. But when all this inefficient
apparatus belongs to a responsible despot, who has been
at pains to publish the social Contract in plain terms:
Aquiescence in my police in return for Security for your-
selves: a great crime has full logical implications. Paris in
a flash heard from attic to cellar that Claude had dug out
of the earth at Pantin from the bloody heap where they
had been packed pell-mell, dead and dying, the pretty
Hortense, eviscerated with a knife; six-year-old Alfred,
torn in the back with a broken haft; Emile and lazy
Henri, strangled with their own mufflers; Achille, quiet
Achille, butchered with a spade; and from the bottom of
the pit, the lamentable Madame Kinck herself, gashed in
fifty places from behind and in front. For the news, Paris
hated its police and its Emperor. What band of apish sav-
ages had the Man of Blood let loose to harry his subjects
now; what new fraud and breach of contract?

The hole at Pantin was a hole in the regime. An un-
countable crowd flowed by gravitation out to it. In one
day it is said a hundred thousand persons passed over
the ploughed field to look at the stained earth. The field
was tramped down so hard by their feet that afterwards
the peasants could not get a plough drawn by a yoke of
oxen through it. Claude had removed the bodies to the
Morgue; the countless crowd itself found the instruments
of the murder in its trampling. A broken kitchen knife, a
pick, a spade, all horribly soiled and clogged. In the pockets of the bodies at the Morgue Claude found a wooden
rosary, seven francs in copper, three clay marbles, tags of

string; and tossed in beside the bodies, a piece of sausage and some crusts, also the little girl's doll.

Inside the coat of Emile was a label, on which was woven the maker's name: Thomas, Roubaix. The police of Roubaix were naturally informed of this.

But before any answer came from them, the proprietor of the Hôtel de Chemin de Fer appeared at the Prefecture and informed them that a woman and five children had called at his establishment the night before the crime, who appeared to answer the description of the victims. This gave the name 'Jean Kinck' to Claude; with this clue the Roubaix police identified the bodies in a short time. All this, which Claude in his Memoirs attempts to pass as a miracle of deductive intelligence, did not deliver to him, nor to the raging Paris crowd which was hourly fed with details by the Press, either the names of the assassins (for it was not believed that one man could have done so much) or the circumstances of the crime. But Claude, who had already composed a theory that this Jean Kinck was one of the guilty (principally because he had disappeared) wired to every seaport in France the bones of his description, drawn from the memories of valets and housemaids at the hotel. In this portrait *parlé,* as it turned out, every detail was false.

This hue and cry for Kinck reached Troppmann at Havre, together with the news of the discovery of his butchery. It is uncertain where he slept the first night; next day he changed his domicile. A tout for the shebeen belonging to a Madame Rouey, named Dourson, found Troppmann wandering about the ropes of the Quai de la

Barre, and entered into conversation. I made every allow-
ance for that natural baseness of witnesses in a *cause
célèbre* that leads them to embroider the evidence with
anything they have learned or thought of that may increase its importance and theirs, but there are things in
Dourson's evidence that he could not have invented. He
states that Troppmann said to him, 'Woe to him who does
me ill, I am a dangerous man.' Also that he intended to
embark for New Orleans, but could not get on board
without a passport. (The Kinck papers were now worse
than useless.) Troppmann accompanied Dourson to his
bouge, where they ate, Troppmann, of course, paying.
Madame Rouey noticed that he had a roll of new five-
franc pieces, Belgian coinage. She offered to change
them for him. Later on Dourson and Troppmann went
out and strolled, and Troppmann talked of his book, the
Wandering Jew. He is clearly past the rabid terror with
which he must have read the news; he is in an intermediate stage. The headlines, the general hysteria of the report
he had read, comforted him much. Though still a fugitive,
and only in danger, this literature gave a foretaste of that
sense of importance, the comfort of notoriety that supports
most murderers in their supposed expiation. He had lost
all but his life and fame.

He felt the need of expansion; this oily rogue Dourson
listened to his bragging, his hints, with notable respect.
Much of what we know of the inner life of Troppmann is
in the evidence of Dourson, an acquaintance of a few
hours. The tout's attentions cumulated the effect of the
newspaper's music. In these moments, aided by the official

hypothesis he read of a gang-murder, Troppmann must have thought out his second lie-world and begun to believe in it. We shall briefly note the principal changes it underwent.

Meanwhile the murderer had registered under the name of 'Fuchs'—a choice that shows how his thoughts were running. With all his might he was thinking himself away from objectivity, romanticizing himself, novelizing himself back into a creature of fiction. The audience of Dourson helped him. They went to sit in a café near the Two Bridges. Troppmann paid again and began to tell the tout the latest details of his story. His name was not Fuchs; it was a much more important one, which no one however could ever learn. He had a rich uncle in America. He was bored of women and pleasures, so he had decided to cross the Atlantic and settle in Texas, 'where the struggle with the elements attracted him.' Nevertheless there were grave reasons why certain high personages did not wish him to go, for he had many secrets; and would Dourson procure for him false papers? Dourson probably agreed.

At this moment a gendarme (Ferrand) strolled in, and caught sight of them. It was his sagacious habit to look at everyone he met with a feint of attention. Troppmann caught the look and had an instinctive recoil. Ferrand had nothing else to do; the café was empty but for them. He went over and asked the uneasy young man his name. Troppmann became very pale and began a story. The gendarme by this time was convinced that he had some dock thief in his hands. He ordered Troppmann to ac-

company him to the police-station. As they walked along
the docks, a wagon drove between them, and in a flash,
with a hundred ghosts at his heels, the murderer bolted.
He ran straight along the jetty, and reaching the end,
threw himself over. In his fall he hit a raft or a buoy,
and from that, dazed, toppled over into the water. The
gendarme and the crowd came running; no one could
swim. At last a caulker, Hauguel, plunged in after the
runaway. He grappled with him at the second dive.
Whether because he was losing consciousness, or because
he wished to drown, Troppmann fought with him, but in
his weakened condition even the muscles that had proved
themselves at Pantin were overcome. He was hauled out
and pumped. The caulker received a gold watch from the
Figaro for his act.

In court, later, the gendarme Ferrand embellished this
fine capture with a story that he had already identified his
prisoner with the Pantin murderer when he escaped. Macé
polishes this story with a fascinating version: that Ferrand's intuition that his prisoner was the missing 'Kinck'
was exactly due to the complete difference of his appearance from the description issued by the Paris police. But
whatever the surprising degree of intelligence shown by
Ferrand, when the inanimate body of the fugitive was
searched all doubts as to their capture were settled. In the
pockets of his grey riding-coat, and in the belt round his
waist, under his shirt, were mortgages, deeds of sale, receipts, private letters, birth certificates in the name of, or
relating to, Jean Kinck and his wife. He had two watches,
one in gold, afterwards identified as the property of Kinck,

one of silver, his own. In a side pocket of his striped
waistcoat lay a pocket-comb which had once summed up
the glorious adventure of travel to young Gustave.

The news that 'Kinck' was found struck Paris like a
universal cerebral explosion. The city was obsessed with
the Pantin case, so deeply that one of the hypotheses that
were being heaped up like clouds by the east wind was
that the whole affair was an invention of the Government
to turn the people's mind from politics. This is a curiosity
of opinion in an over-sharp population which recurred
under almost exactly the same form during the Clemenceau dictature in the Landru case. In reality, the murders
of Troppmann brought the most terrible damage to the
Imperial regime, and prepared in no subtle way the minds
of the French for the complete disaffection that appeared
after the matter of Sedan. To the undeveloped masses, it
seemed a portent of national disasters, an omen in the old
Roman way, which indeed the swift course of events was
to fulfil. Old women in farthest villages shook their bonnets over the monstrosity and prophesied mighty judg-
ments of God on the times. But these extremes of the
simplest and the slyest were but tributaries of the main
effect of the event on the psychology of the nation. The
collapse of Troppmann's ignoble dream pulled with it
the immense and unstable structure of the Spirit of the
times, into which it was interlocked. Thousands no doubt
of those who visited the hole in the field took their girls
and their wine, and made it an outing. But hundreds of
thousands more, in every station of life, fathers and
mothers, felt that this but increased a massive feeling of
disgust, for the times, for the lesser villainies committed

daily by and against them in the ferocious hunt for wealth, and by natural transit for the police, the regime, the court of sick scoundrels and 'arrivers' to whom they traced its root. Troppmann made the bourgeois realize that he was sick of the epoch. He disillusioned them almost more than he terrified them. From that date the last cord with which the bogus Napoleon held his subjects, the consolation of law and order, was worn out.

If Troppmann had any more skill in fiction than the ordinary mass-murderer there was a chance of safety for him in this general mood. From the beginning it is evident that the public wanted to believe him. They accepted his first clumsy subterfuge of passing for Kinck; in the first scattering of the hunt they were chasing Kinck, not Troppmann. Every later version of his stories they made efforts to swallow, only rejecting them, with reluctance, when their possibility could by no means be gulped down. They had ceased to believe in the Empire; they did their best to believe in Troppmann. Claude himself, and Macé, all the policemen of the epoch, give an inkling of this attitude of the respectable man-in-the-street, when they show in their memoirs that in spite of all, in spite of Troppmann's confessed false confessions, in spite of all evidence, they themselves still believed years afterwards that there were attenuating secrets behind the murderer, complicities, motives that they regret will never be cleared up, because the dossiers of the case were burned in the Commune. But Troppmann with all his like, living more intensely in fiction than honest men, and being indeed principally distinguished from them by that stigma, are also always miserably deficient in powers of invention. It is as if deprived of sympathy, first condition of all crime from pilfering to homicide, the roots of imagination are withered in them, and the wretched twig of self-hypnotization is all that remains in their clutch.

Troppmann in prison, saved from howling crowds by good walls and gratings, sets himself till his nerves crack to build a shelter of lies. But art, even of story-telling, needs more vital energy than sufficed to disembowel and bury a little girl beside her mother. Each of his productions was poorer than the last. Divide them for clearness into two. First, he states that Jean Kinck with his son Gustave, suspecting his wife of adultery, himself filled the hole at Pantin, Troppmann 'merely' looking on. Two days afterwards, in the same field, a few yards distant from his mother's grave, the body of Gustave is found, mangled by the same hand as hers.

Second, Troppmann can only add, lamentably, that it was Jean Kinck himself who killed even Gustave. That he had disguised this detail out of human respect for the father.

On this feeble monstrosity he stays for some weeks, until the body of Kinck is found, in a shallow hole under the ruins of Herrenfluch, on his own indication. The police hopelessly failing in finding the body, had bethought themselves of importing Madame Troppmann *mère* into the cell, and she (I know not quite with what idea relatives follow in such cases) induced her son to reveal the exact spot of his first crime. Analysis, made possible by the impurities left by the home-made prussic acid of Troppmann, had no difficulty in proving that Kinck had been poisoned.

Not to be beaten even now, after a week's brain-twisting he came to the story of accomplices, with which he should have begun. This, after its remodeling by his defender Maître Lachaud, the last of the Romantic barristers, took some consistency. One passage in Lachaud's speech for the defence will sum it up, and deliver us from the mass of contradictory detail and retouching with which Troppmann himself bungled it.

'How could a single assassin have accomplished such a work in the conditions of time and space at his disposal? At five o'clock he buys the tools from the ironmonger; he came back to get them at eight o'clock. At nine o'clock he arrives at Quartre Chemins. Now, from that point to the hole that was dug is more than six hundred metres. This grave, what is its size? It was three metres long, forty centimetres deep, sixty centimetres wide. Tell me how much time should it take to dig such a hole? Then the murderer had to return to the Nord Railway Station; what time was it then? Coachman Bardot will tell you: "It was 10.50 when they got into my carriage." How in so short a time could Troppmann have been to the field, dug the grave, and returned to the station? When he says, "I had accomplices who prepared the grave and when I got there it was ready," is there not something there that ought to strike you?

'Let us continue. Troppmann takes the carriage at 10.50. He gets down with the mother and two children; they have to walk from Quatre Chemins to the place where the hole is dug—550 to 600 metres; then, after the three victims have had their throats cut, he comes back: again 600 metres. How long did he take? Twenty minutes, says the coachman.'

To this physical doubt the defence clung with desperation. Every time (or every time his brain thought of it
quickly enough) that one of the witnesses spoke (it was
rare) of his having been seen in the company of another
unidentified person, Troppmann would rise and throw to
the judge with all his anxious self-deception: 'It was one
of my accomplices; the long one, the short one.' But was
the limit necessarily so extraordinary as Maître Lachaud
made out? Taking his obviously outside figures—the
coachman's twenty minutes is only a guess—Troppmann
in that time had gone over a thousand yards, half walking,
half running, and killed a woman and two babies, not one
of whom seems to have been capable of resistance, in the
time. It is quick; with what we know of Troppmann's
athletic powers, with what we surmise of his rabid ferocity, it does not seem out of the question. Re-reading the
horrible medical evidence, it seems credible that he bat-
tered the first batch wildly, possibly the affair of a few
seconds, then ran back, controlling his breath so that his
hurry should not be remarked, took the three remaining
boys back, and simultaneously throttling the two eldest by
their scarves, which he held in his right hand, killed or
silenced the smallest with one blow of his left. It is not
certain or necessary that the first group should have been
quite dead when he returned. It would even appear more
likely that he left them lying in a heap and was obliged
to end the little girl on his return. The very ferocity, the
blindness of the blows points to the work of one man.
What, we might ask in Lachaud's oratorical way, Do you
imagine that men able to take their time would have so
mangled the bodies? And to his traditional question, which

every defender asks in every hopeless case, Can any man, or boy of twenty, ever have existed capable of such a horror? we must reply sternly, Do you imagine that there is any other way possible to butcher a woman and children than a blind, mad slashing and smashing? Or that Troppmann or any other villain could have killed a whole family at a time without hypnotizing himself while he did it that he had before him so many trees to hew, so many pieces of senseless wood to splinter? Do you suppose that there is any sane mind that could stand such a scene if it were done slowly, with mercy or thought of suffering?

For the rest, the Crown Prosecutor (Grandperret) has the last word. 'Who lured Kinck to Alsace? Troppmann. Who wrote to him? Troppmann. Who met him at Bollwiller? Troppmann. Who alone was seen with Kinck at Soultz? Troppmann. Who bought the bottle of wine in which the poison was placed? Troppmann. It is the prisoner who is everywhere in the case, always alone. He makes the poison, he administers it, he draws Gustave to Alsace, he is last seen with him in Paris. He buys the spades, he visits the field, it is he who knows its emplacement from his stay in the neighbourhood, as he knows the Castle of Herrenfluch. It is he who puts Madame Kinck into the coach, he who takes her hand into the shadows of that night, he who returns to fetch the rest to their death. And it is he again who secures all the spoils, the money of Kinck, the money of Madame Kinck, the papers, the watches, down to the very pocket-comb. It is Troppmann who is guilty alone.'

Yet in spite of this decisive conclusion, the public, avid to believe *something,* to replace something in the

growing void of its agnosticism, continued to murmur ap-
provingly every time that Troppmann threw up his long
arms and broke into the evidence with a charge against
his 'accomplices.' The very police, as we have seen, shared
the superstition about them; and men in high places long
afterwards hinted mysteriously that behind Troppmann
was a spy case, a fragment of the schemes of Bismarck in
Alsace. These latter legends have too familiar a brand
upon them for us, who have lived through the last war,
to rouse anything but a cautious smile. Concede that
Troppmann had friends of his own sort in Paris among
the wild band of unemployable Germans at Pantin, men
indeed whose existence gave Troppmann's rickety imagination the leg upon which to prop his stories. But men
whom none, least of all Troppmann, was ever able to
name. To the step of the guillotine indeed he clung to this
last story; that there were three Alsatians in the business,
master hands, whom he had met by accident years before
while they were in the act of committing a robbery. They
were the counterfeiters, they were the principal guilty
ones. Who are they? Troppmann could not say, grave
motives, noble motives, nailed his lips. But in a clump of
furze, six inches beneath the soil, near Herrenfluch in
Alsace, was buried the letter-case containing all their
names. . . . The police actually searched for this will-o'-
the-wisp; they never found it, for Troppmann alone could
take them in person to the place. In the hope of escape
in his native thickets, said the prosecution; in no such a
thought-out idea, say we; but simply that this last pitiful
fiction was the bottom of his store, which he held to, yes,

as little Achille held to his stump of sausage. Troppmann
could not face the supreme catastrophe without a belief,
even in the butt end of one of his own lies.

So he slowly progresses over that road whose ruts are
always the same to all the wretches who have passed on it
and are to pass, the shameful last days of a condemned
man. He feels, like the others, the strong spirits of the
trial days, the breath of importance, the exhilarating eminence of being a public show. He, too, traverses the un-
holy weeks, the feverish days of hope and the terror of
drowsy nights alone with the guards. He too surprised
everyone by moments of boredom, when a joke gave him
pleasure; by feeling human hunger, thirst, vanity. His
family never visited him again.

His appeal to the Emperor, which Lachaud took the
trouble of forwarding for him, was inevitably refused.
On the 19th of January, before it was dawn, the executioner is ready. He, and the Governor of the Prison of La
Roquette, an unending file of personalities and journalists swarm into Troppmann's cell. The strait-jacket is taken
off. Troppmann is dressed, according to the use, in the
clothes he wore when arrested. The neck of his shirt is
cut with cold shears. He is pinioned so that his chest is
forcibly thrown out like a guardsman's on parade; his feet
tied so that he has to walk with mincing steps. Death is
allowed by Regulation to seize him only an inch at a time.
He was then pushed and edged across the stone yard,
through a door into the first freshness of the morning
and a vast activity which made him blink as if he had
hobbled into a glare. The triangle of the Roquette is an

orgy. Men and women, countless and indistinguishable in the fading street-lamps, are eating, kissing, singing, bawling, drunk, laughing, cold and angry. As the roped man totters through the door, moving his feet in a nauseous sort of industry, the crowd lay down their occupations and, as if they are all in some tremendous practical joke, they roar and point at him. As if the walls had nudged them they sway and fall down and grab each other to keep their feet. The black window-sills of the low-class hotels are bulging with men in evening dress and half-naked women who wave bottles at him and scuffle. The transition from the lugubrious enclosure to this ocean of mouths startles the murderer, and the obstacle to his instinctive movement of recoil of his cords and the inexorably shoving men round him, turn his fright into hysteria. At the same moment the priest, who has walked backwards in front of him with a crucifix held up to hide the machine, moves to one side. In full view he sees the oblong shadow of the motionless thing. The men who are jostling him close in as he violently throws himself back, force him with their knees and hands up each step of the ladder. He tries to catch his toes in the rungs. At the top a shabby man in a frock-coat is waiting; Troppmann stumbles on the last rung and falls flat on a board, that tips him with sickening surprise under the knife. He foams and bites and throws back his head; Claude says his strength was such that he saw the knife before it fell.

The
Self-Help
of
G. J. Smith

Sir,
   In answer to your application my parentage and
age &c. My mother was a Buss horse, my father a
Cab driver my sister a Roughrider over the Artic
regions, my brothers were all galant sailors on a
steam-roller.

G. J. SMITH

WE HAVE BUT LITTLE TO SET AGAINST THIS CLAIM OF
George Joseph Smith to be the issue of a phantasmagoria
and not a human family. His birth certificate states that
he was born at 92 Roman Road, Bethnal Green, London,
on the 11th January 1872. His father, the 'Cab Driver,'
according to this meagre document was also an insurance agent: an insecure category that may (risking
something on the observed unspontaneity of a mass-murderer's imagination) include the practice of flower and
figure painting, which, in one of his marriage explanations, George Joseph claimed for him. Beyond this cloudy
genealogy, it is vain to seek. The very surname is clue-
less, for all family trees lose themselves among the Smiths.
If ants have names for each other, they must use a tiny
equivalent for Smith. It has no handle for the curious to
meddle with. It is a name unlimited by space or time, it is
an anonymity that may cover an earl or a gipsy evangelist,

and a sort of evasion of the laws of heredity. 'Smith' suited
the fantastic figure of this man who hated identification.
With it, his only heirloom, he could wander undetectably
in the depths of any directory; he could enjoy some of
the privilege of the disembodied spirit. He escapes the
unplatonic ties of family, and promotes himself out of commonplace crime to the company of Mr. Hyde, and Spring-
Heeled Jack; a phantasm haunting the hinder terraces of
the Lower Middle Class, a subject for a new Tale of Wonder and Imagination, where, instead of Hermits, are Respectable Spinsters; instead of Dungeons, the shadows of
boarding-house basements; instead of skulls, a more grue-
some terror of Tin Baths.

From the obscure bourn from which he came to his
first appearance in the light of record is nine years. Our
knowledge of this first appearance is solely due to his
own negligent confidence to a woman in days before his
character had set. At nine years old he was sent to a reformatory, where he stayed until he was sixteen. Meagre
as it is, the information has many implications. A reformatory boy is indeed seldom different from other boys when
he goes in. When he comes out, he is a type. It is a
punishment for acts which proverbially—and in certain
classes of society, practically, are recognized as natural to
the growing male: theft, cruelty, various destructions of
property. In the complicated social system of England
there is a contradictory attitude towards this phenomenon.
If the family is rich, it is excused, or in certain circumstances even praised as natural and a sign of health. Thus
the theft of growing fruit, the breaking of windows or
fences is not only pardoned, but often encouraged by jocu-

lar reminiscence and approving laughter. Graver deeds are punished privately by the family. When the family is poor, or only callous, the boy who was taken in any such act (in Smith's days) was certain of from four to seven years' imprisonment in a reformatory. An apple off a barrow, a stone through a window, a broken street lamp: any of these acts may have brought on Smith his sentence. If he had been out of his teens, such offences would have entailed a fine or a few weeks' hard labour. But for philanthropic reasons such leniency is considered against the interests of the growing boy, if he is poor, and it is usual to send him to imprisonment for such period of his boyhood as may remain. This imprisonment of course was quite different from that inflicted on the adult; in addition to the manual work of prisons, the reformatory boy had to work at his books, and while there was no ticket-of-leave or remission system for good behaviour, corporal punishment, practically abolished for the grown prisoner, was an important part of the reformatory method for the youngsters. This system, devised for the betterment of the lower classes, the correction of their faults and to assist them to bring up their families hard-working members of the State, does not always succeed. The boys on their release may be divided into two categories: those who have either outgrown the destructive stage without damage to property in their confinement, or whom the wholesome lesson of the power of the forces of order has discouraged from ever again trying to oppose it; and those who from a feeling of revolt, or because of hereditary tares, are incorrigible and henceforth for the rest of their days are integrally attached to the police system as criminals.

The first class are set to the credit side of our system; they are assured that no stigma attaches to them for their past, and all they have to do is to persuade a trades union to recognize their irregular apprenticeship in the reformatory workshop and admit them to the practice of the trade they have been taught. The second class are our failure; nothing more can be done for them. But they may be certain that their future sentences will usually be longer than those given to other criminals who have not had advantages to excuse them.

Smith, we can detect from circumstantial evidence, particularly his correspondence, left the Reformatory in a state somewhat intermediary between reclamation and total loss. He was certainly neither cowed nor inspired sufficiently to make his peace with society. But unlike the majority of 'bad cases,' he had used his head during the seven years, and had learnt something important and useful beyond the beggarly R's and the amateur woodwork. He was released with a precise knowledge of the ethics, and even of the vocabulary, of that good world that governs reformatories. Where else than from a good-hearted clerical visitor could he have learnt to compose such a sentence, 'I vow to take advantage of every future day that the great powers have ordained, until the miserable past is absolutely outlived and a character established which will be worthy of your appreciation.' Or 'Possibly many years are before us all wherein peace and goodwill will always keep the past at bay, and a Christian brotherly feeling established.' This peak-faced urchin from Bethnal Green has remembered word for word, almost to the intonation, what he heard on Sundays from his spiritual father, even to the characteristic nervous shrinking from New Testament onomatology. Certainly the young delinquent did something more than pick his nose during these seven years of reformation. He had acquired what no foreigner can ever hope to do, the practice of that difficult English undenominationalism under which our State Christianity hides itself against the double onslaught of the Education Act and Higher Criticism. He had mastered the right tone in which to speak of the past, the attitude towards the future expected of one on whom so much State money had been spent. In fact the root theory of reform was in him. Of all his studies, the concept of 'making good,' social atonement in its simplest form—to make a good living out of reach of the law—was the firmest embedded. As to the way to achieve it, he had not been so well instructed. The only rule he retained of this latter part of the curriculum was that an alibi, moral, local, or historical, always requires two witnesses.

With this baggage—it might have made him a masterly writer of begging-letters—he had also acquired at some time in between the imperceptible chinks of ceaseless routine one of those devastating egoisms, with which, whether they arise out of fear or vice, all mass-murderers are afflicted. Besides their habit of living in a constructed lie, besides the lust of killing which is a mysterious but constant symptom, this damned class are invariably selfish to a degree of which the greatest actor can have no conception: passions that can be more justly compared with that of a mother for a sickly child than with any lesser love between the sexes. Such egotisms are not the growth of a day, nor within the reach of anyone who has not searched the bottom of possible miseries. To love oneself like a Troppmann or Smith is a lifelong paroxysm in which the adoration of Saint John of the Cross, the jealousy of Othello, the steadfastness of a Dante is imitated; if there were a measure of intensity, I would dare say excelled. In other forms of love admiration may be a necessary factor. The love of a Smith for himself needs no such prop. It absorbs every globule of his being, so that when it is present God and Man alike have no part in him. His self-compassion, self-pity, wakened by what self-knowledge of wretchedness we do not know, sucked the meaning out of every existence but his own. In the life of Burke we suspected it. In the story of Troppmann we deduced its growth; in the case of Smith we see this demoniac Narcissism itself.

From the day of his release for two years Smith's history runs quite underground again. But there are two manholes. In 1890 he serves a week's imprisonment for a petty theft. In 1891 a London Court sent him to six months' hard labour for stealing a bicycle—at that time a luxury peculiarly seductive to a young man of nineteen. Then the trace of his woes and adventures disappears entirely. Possibly he had enlisted. There is some vague allusion to Army Service in what his first wife remembered of his confidences; and once he claimed to a boarding-house keeper to have been a gymnasium instructor. There was some vague allure of the corporal about his walk; some trace of pipe-clay and the button-stick about his later elegance. His unnaturally tough biceps were shaped by some other process than ordinary toil.

Then comes another official memento of his crooked track, the most important since the record of the Reformatory. In 1896, in the name of George Baker, he received twelve months' hard labour for larceny and receiving. This event is strictly analogous to the breaking of the cocoon that frees the fully-grown night-moth. The man has separated himself definitely from the caterpillar that was G. J. Smith, to begin a series of lives in other names, each separate in environment both personal and local and only joined by the hidden chain of his own identity. A double life is not enough for him: henceforth he will make of every year, sometimes every month, a separate life, in which his own history, his name, his profession, as well as the set of personages in which it is spent, are completely changed. He has embarked on a serial adventure in which each episode is complete in itself, whose master-plot is known only to himself; a life divided into impervious compartments. Other men may have mysteries in their life— every incident in his was a separate secret.

This development is simultaneous to his discovery of Woman. Every criminal out of his teens sooner or later collides with the Riddle of Women, and his fate depends, more critically than that of honest men, on the answer he gives it. He may be tangled in the sentimental obstruction of a woman who fears the code, and then be caught in one of the three perilous policies of taciturnity, desperation or reformation. If she is of the same turn he has to share her dangers, and double his own. But if he has even a part of the exalted egotism of Smith he is more surely doomed. He will then try to use women. He will embark on the forbidden and hopeless enterprise of exploiting all this ore lying to his hand: half humanity, with half humanity's property and all humanity's spending. It is a grave moment in life when it suddenly appears that the ranks of the enemy are not solid; that besides men who fight, punish, resist, there are also women who may be persuaded to love. It is the moment also, if he but knew it, to rush back into the thick of the battle and, doing and receiving evils that he understands, continue open war. All music is there to warn him, the prickings of his own blood, the recesses of his earliest memory, that here is a temple in which sacrilege is desperately dangerous. But this outlying Smith, or George Baker, has no caution. From the day he met his first woman, he set eagerly to exploit her. Somewhere in the tunnel he had developed the canaille virility of a Guardsman whose odour, heightened by hair pomade, blacking and tobacco, lures women out of the kitchen like a pack after aniseed. After a short fumbling with the elementary difficulties of their jealousies and timidity, he had his first team of hussies at work for him: their part being to pilfer from their masters and hand over the goods. We do not know what blunder led to the first failure of the scheme. The method, not the idea, was afterwards improved.

In this first essay Smith had come to taste, probably for the first time in his life, the strongest mental pleasure in our civilization, the joys of property. They are peculiarly dangerous to a man of his type. Even the minute quantity of superfluity that his love-slaves put into their master's hands intoxicated him. He had always before lived on the bread-line. None of his earnings had lasted longer than the shortest way from hand to mouth. His first exploitation of women opened to him a new world, garnished with reserve stores against the bitter surprises of life. It furnished his imagination with savings-bank books, cash-boxes, and money laid by. New avenues opened beyond him at the end of which shimmered title-deeds, script, fascinating intrinsically and still more in the promise they contained of the final salvation of his only darling, his adored, his own self.

The tiger had tasted blood; or just as accurately George Joseph had experienced conversion, from the despairing vagrancy of a prison-dweller on leave, to a life of hopeful motive. Smith was a born possessor. The mere routine of acquisition sensually excited him. He picked up the jargon of property law as the Renaissance learned Greek, with the meticulous enthusiasm of a grammarian. Women, even when they kill, always give something. In his first brush with them he brought back that hobby of the lonely, that consolation of the fearful: Avarice. In its strange and twisted ways the neophyte was at once expert.

On his release he appeared in Leicester eager to begin his first hoard. We have mislaid the chain of little reasons that made him open a sweet-shop. But we are allowed for a long time to watch him through a plate-glass window, serving children bulls'-eyes and all the assortment of morsels of aniline and sugar for which they wait from Saturday to Saturday in modern towns; or paper bags of broken biscuits and cake refuse; enjoying a till and a lease; practicing himself, as if they were sonnets, in the pretty art of writing business letters, with Re and Yours to hand, acknowledging kind receipts and begging to state.

But after closing hours when the last shelf had been counted and tidied, he would sally out with his chest rigidly squared in search for more women, to see if they had any more to give him. So he came upon one Caroline Thornhill and married her in the symbolic name of George Oliver Love. In his marriage declaration, he promoted his father to one of the most eminent ranks in society that he knew, that of detective.

But if every incipient miser was a business man, the banks would shut their paying desks. Love and Company were bankrupt in six months. The only asset saved was Mrs. Caroline Love. He took her to London and set her to work, after his first manner. He attended to the postal and receiving departments, that is he wrote letters of recommendation to employers for her and took what she stole from them.

In the course of this business he came to discover the seaside. It delighted him. From Brighton they went to Hove, from Hove to Hastings, finding everywhere business easier, people more gullible. Smith had found his America. Everywhere around him were rolling prairies of single women, so tame that the hunting male could approach them with the wind. This English seaside has not been methodically explored, yet it is as fascinating in its way as the labyrinths of the vast industrial towns of which it is a sub-continent. The scheme is different, the manner of life and customs are different. Instead of the regular pulse of nine hours between factory and tenement, the regular circulation of the traffic arteries that pump the crowd fresh and living into the vessels of production in the early morning, and the network of veins that conducts their sluggish stream back to the sleeping cells at night, soiled, fatigued, at the seaside there are two other steady tides, at ten o'clock and four, towards the sea. To enable hundreds of thousands to look at the water at the same time, it has been fitted with a T-shaped road, made up of a concrete walk along the shore, and an iron and concrete jetty, a shorter arm, jutting at right angles into the sea. At the end of this jetty is a round glass booth of great size which is the point of concentration of the whole life of the town. Here music of a special kind is performed: songs in which lifelong love is praised, and marches and dances. At the back of the towns the downs have been trimmed and small plots of grass planted for the game of golf. In many places other plots of land have been fenced off for the other game of lawn-tennis. In these two amusements the majority of the better-class visitors pass their time, sometimes waiting for long periods for an opportunity to play. But in the lesser world of Smith these artificial distractions fill small place; most of its time is spent in the morning and afternoon walk on the sea-roads, or in station round the official music and the private choirs that are spaced along the main-road and the shore.

With these changed institutions of seaside life naturally goes a large alteration of social custom. The rigid observance of the English social code, a variety largely influenced by ascetic Christianity as well as by climatic, feudal and other conditions, depends so much on mutual policing that the slightest removal from the circle where he is known and by which his conduct is ruled produces a considerable relaxation in behaviour of the normal Englishman; and still more in that of the normal Englishwoman.

This dissolvent comes into play in the seaside holiday, which like the annual orgy of many African tribes, the majority of our population periodically observes. It is a counterpart of the bodily release from the abominable round of drudgery to which the nation, by an unhappy development, is for the most part condemned, whose only intermission is this yearly visit to the free air of the sea. Once a year we must have leisure to breathe smokeless air. Probably the temporary abandonment of the corset of the innumerable niceties of conduct is as necessary to our naturally adventurous, unconventional, and even lyrical race as the physical relief.

In this world Smith, for the first time introduced by the hazard of his business, felt so suited that he seldom afterwards operated elsewhere. He perceived the extraordinary advantage, to a man working irregularly and out of the organization, of a *milieu* in which freedom from work is the rule, discretion and change of identity conventional, and where sudden comings and goings cause no remark. But he had particularly noticed the possibilities of the changed rules of conduct among the women. In London, or even on Sunday nights in Leicester, their approach was always difficult, often impossible. But at the seaside, provided a minimum of *nous,* that principal barrier between the sexes—the need of a formal introduction—was down. Further, those venerated guardians of British morality, the board and lodging house and hotel keepers, are disarmed at the seaside. This law of liberty stretching in depth as well as area, not only was his power of action on the servile class of women he had known hitherto greatly enlarged, but another stratum of the sex, higher and therefore richer than anything he had aspired to, was here within his reach. His first turn on the glistening promenades convinced him of this. But before we can follow him in his new discovery, we must press him back again, like a jack-in-the-box, into his cell for another two years hard labour. Mrs. Love had ended the second episode in the usual way.

Silvio Pellico, Baron Trenck and half a score other innocent and learned men have informed us of their sufferings in prison life. But, that I know of, no genuine thief has published his impressions of confinement. Yet there must be a difference of view, if only because the latter must be deprived of the moral snobbery that so comforted Pellico. From such observations (usually facetious!) as we find strayed among the memoirs of prison governors and the like, it would appear that there are three periods in the course of a long sentence: first, when the guilty prisoner is crushed with despair and hardly able to live; second, when the routine soothes, and the time-shortening effect of monotony emerges; third, when the man begins to count, and the long chagrin of calendar-crossing sets in. Conscripts know this abominable occupation; schoolboys know it. In any old barracks the plasterers find little sums pencilled on the walls: so many days endured, so many to come before '*la classe.*' And insomniacs know, what convicts in their last months know, the precise length of an hour, the speed of the minute-hand. Perhaps these degrees are well known to all judges and enter into their standards for measuring the days, months, years, they apportion with such easy assurance to any variety of guilt. But the enormous mental constructions that men, by nature ungeared with reàlity, must be rearing in the silence of four walls, the strange and idiotic plans they must make in such a waking dream, we can only guess at. Happiest certainly of all those who, like Love, doing his 730 days for theft by receiving from his wife, have walled up along with them all that they adore, if it is only their wretched selves.

He was released in 1902, to find that Mrs. Love had fled to Canada. He must have pondered much on this circumstance, for a voyage to Canada becomes henceforth an integral ornament of his lies. Possibly he tried to make up his mind to follow her, seeing no other way of making a living, for one forgets more than one learns in a cell. But gradually what he had observed at the seaside came back to him; then he bethought himself of other women, more convenient to his hand. He left the Canadian voyage lying in his mental life, complete enough for him to have a working belief in its accomplishment ever afterwards; and returned to the exploitation of other women.

In 1899 he already had conquered his first middle-class spinster; perhaps this was one of the reasons for Mrs. Love's denunciation. She was a boarding-house keeper in London, whom he met at the seaside. He married her at once, and some time after his release returned to her. When she was sucked dry, he went on to others. For eight years he proceeded from spinster to spinster, leaving behind him a litter of closed savings-bank accounts. Some he got rid of at once, who bored or irritated him, by a set technique of taking them to a public exhibition, pretexting a bodily need that would separate them for a minute, and disappearing. Some were worth the troublesome business of marriage; for some the promise sufficed. Smith led in these years a leisured life. He began to frequent public libraries, and soon was praising himself for his literary taste. Some mysterious reminiscence of his father gave him a peg for believing he was an innate connoisseur of the arts. He indulged this talent by allowing himself a certain sum for buying an occasional piece of old furniture, which he would afterwards sell, and stood such losses as he met with in this traffic with equanimity. Second-hand dealing brought him in direct touch with more women. It satisfied his pride and fed his real business.

In 1908 as an incident in another episode, the details of which are totally lost, he became for a few weeks a servant in a West End Club, then was dismissed for inefficiency. The next year with some £90, the largest gain he had yet made—it came from a Brighton conquest—he adventured to Bristol, and there opened a second-hand shop. For some time the idea of a settled base, as far as possible from London, without being out of reach of the hunting grounds of the coast, had occurred to him. Here he married his next-door neighbour, a Miss Pegler, marking the special nature of the union and his intention to make it permanent, by using the name of Smith.

Sooner or later Smith was bound to arrive at this end. Even the foxes need a base. It was the necessary complement of that hoard whose quest always now obsessed him. It would be a hiding-place in case of need, and the necessary fixed point from which he could estimate the pleasures and pains of his episodic adventures. He did not intend to make it more. He told Miss Pegler besides the customary fable of his rich aunt, the truth that he intended to carry on his business of travelling about the country, with sundry warnings against curiosity, which she usually dutifully heeded. But from the foundation of this little fort henceforward directly developed the plot of his fate. These fantastic creatures of reverie, as long as they do not meddle with the humdrum of the world, seem for a time safe. But as soon as they leave the air, their story begins its last inevitable chapters. It is the phase which we have seen at its acute form in Burke, when confident in his security he had got to a pitch of madness, a stage at which Troppmann toys insolently with a whole family that he counts already dead and done with, when a deep illusion of relief takes possession of them and they stand-down the sentries. In Smith this feeling of confidence took the form of founding this home-base with a wife in Bristol, both a feature of his life of petty swindler, which it capped and ended, and the first stage of his career of murder, which it began.

For with a home, Smith indulged himself in another of his dreams; he bought his first house. The superfluity that began with his first use of women had grown to a hoard of £240, which he used towards the purchase price of a cottage in Southend, whither, giving up the Bristol shop, they then removed. At last he could enjoy title-deeds, the process of transfer, the full consciousness of possession. It spoiled him for work. This was no Casanova, drawn by an everlasting curiosity and passion to seek new women all his life. Smith, like all his class of women-exploiters, was nothing but a lady-killer, a man essentially monogamous, whom sexual novelty inwardly disgusts and repels, who persists in the hunt only for the money or boasting it can give him. It may be that an intuition of this kernel of monogamy in these false Don Juans is the sting or the prize that makes their success. Sensuality in both sexes is as rare as a real passion for rare foods, or wines, or jewels. Smith, having his property and his Pegler, stayed at home in his own house. He fell into a shirt-sleeve life, and in the evening, instead of a lingering promenade past basement grids, or along sea-fronts, he would sit over a dish of sausages or potter with paint and nails, saving money, not making it. His great pleasure was to go over the grocer's book and feel the head of a family. Occasionally he would visit the Saturday afternoon auctions and listen knowingly to the remarks of the dealers, or drop in to a workman's flat just to take a look at a sideboard that had been in the family for years. But saving halfpennies on the kitchen bills by itself will not pay them. In spite of all his niggling thrift at length Smith was forced to let the house and go back to lodgings in Bristol, then to raise money on his sacred deeds on mortgage from the Woolwich Insurance Company from whom he had bought it. The raising of these first loans gave him so much pleasure in the officialism, the documents, testimonies, receipts, application forms they entailed, that he almost missed their disagreeable meaning. When the money was spent he roused himself for another raid on the women. With temper, as a man is aroused from sleep on a cold morning. Pegler and his next victim had to know it.

It was not necessary for him, it proved, to journey to his usual grounds by the seaside. In Bristol itself, somewhere in an evening walk, in the bare street, or under trees by some forlorn cricket-ground—I do not know—he brushed acquaintance with Bessie Constance Annie Mundy. She was then thirty-three years old, a full spinster, of that unhappy breed plentiful in late Victorian families. A full and critical study of her class, like that of most other phases of English social life of the nineteenth-early-twentieth century, has not yet been made, though their bizarre originality will doubtless tempt many an investigator in future centuries. Here will suffice a brief muster of general characteristics, in order to explain the fall of Miss Mundy to the power of Smith, and to a certain extent the seemingly impossible, but in reality very frequent, liability of the Mundy class to the Smith class. Fundamentally, though not obtrusively, the class of women to which she belonged was an economic product of the immense days of English trade, which beginning coincidentally with the downfall of the French Empire created a huge new middle-class. The absorption of this into the rudimentary *schema* of the English eighteenth-century aristocracy forms practically the whole of the modern social history of our race and its institutions. The men of this new bourgeoisie were somewhat easily assimilated to the elder, petty gentry of the country, who with a beautiful tolerance, unknown in any other country and which in its earliest stages excited the contemptuous wonder of Napoleon Bonaparte (ever a snob), received them as readily if not as eagerly as Early Christian Missionaries baptized the Goths into civilization. The generic title of nobility, 'gentleman,' was extended to them with such philosophical and ethical explanations—and notably false etymology—as made the process plausible. Accepted as spiritual equals, the neophytes pressed their assimilation earnestly in manners and ways of thought. The mercantile gentlemen sent their sons to these special schools with which the Renaissance had equipped the country gentlemen, schools specifically designed to the needs of this latter, where, by internal discipline and the almost exclusive study of the classics, the English lesser noblesse had been raised, if not to the cultural level of the French, at any rate far above that of the rough clodhoppers and Junkers of other northern countries. In this unlikely melting-pot the new-comers lost many of the qualities that had made their fathers' fortunes, in exchange for a culture which at its highest adds something Greek to the common round of rustic amusements and tasks. As far as the lowest borders of the middle-class the ideal, in short, became the country gentleman; and instead of a sharp, spectacled exporter with a pen over his ear, the popular image of England became that bluff, prosperous English squire, John Bull. Only one of the consequences of this development interests us: its effect on the status of women, and particularly on the creation of that class or order, the English genteel spinster. The English Squire, for whom the quasi-totality of Englishmen who could read and write now strove to be mistaken, had the ascetic views on women natural to an open-air, uncourtly life, and this accordingly became the standard of the middle-class of the nation. The brother had become a gentleman, the sister, naturally, a lady. If the boy had to pretend that the shot-gun was his main tool and not a pen, though his high stool, six days in the week, was his only hunter, the girls had to perform the far more difficult make-believe of being the châtelaines of the gloomy town houses their fathers necessarily continued to live in, and model their conduct, their outlook, their ways upon that of fortunate prototypes who had fields, servitors, gardens, and all the multifarious occupations of the country-side. As direct consequence sprang into existence a class of women who had nothing to do, whom their chosen norm of behaviour forbade anything which would differentiate them from their country model, and thus 'be unladylike.' Barred from Court and salon, as well as hunt-meet and the still-room, they were bereft of any reason for existence, except the passive wait for marriage. But not all could marry. From time to time (it is one of the strongest fascinations of the English nineteenth century) educators and reformers sought to fill this vacuum. The most notable of them, Ruskin, inspired these middle-class spinsters to a doughty attempt to interest themselves in Art, particularly Italian and Mediæval Art, which has lasted almost until our own days. In that pre-war year with which we are concerned there had finally evolved a type out of all these influences to which Miss Mundy and thousands of others rigorously conformed. Over a superfluity, a complete uselessness, if such a word can be applied with a full sense of sympathy and pity, as no Stamboul odalisque ever was useless, they had bravely trained a tenuous decoration of books, and tastes and principles: the *Rosary* and Tosti's *Good-Bye,* and *Sesame and Lilies,* with Way-Farer Anthologies and Botticelli prints, and limp-leather editions of the poets, with fifty other like motives, which in their combination have a certain, essentially tragic, poise. For underneath the garland was a misery and a lack, all the more tormenting because in most cases it was unconscious and undefined, for that Reality, which three generations of fantastic theorizing of men had in no way disposed of. Some of them escaped it by working in the one ironical way possible to Ladies, by educating another generation of girls to their own sad situation. But thousands more, like Miss Mundy, whose circumstances allowed of it, carried their load of meaningless days and years wherever hazard took them, over the whole of England and to watering-places, boarding-houses and pensions over the western half of Europe. The loveless, superfluous middle-class spinster is that institution round which George Joseph Smith, that other typical product of our civilization, has for some time been prowling.

The father of Miss Mundy was a bank manager in a country town, an intelligent and capable man who left his daughter a comfortable legacy of £2,500. This sum, invested and controlled by her uncle, produced £8 a month and some small additional fraction, which he held as a reserve for her. It sufficed for a simple life which she spent in various boarding-houses up and down the country, passing from one to the other at the hazard of the season or the movements of her friends. She was a tall, educated woman, extremely reserved, who accepted her nomadic fate, her daily round of perfectly meaningless acts, outwardly with complete resignation. Into such a life, in which the only object is to stay 'respectable,' the intrusion of a Smith is almost supernatural. It is as if through the gate of a quiet convent, in the hours of the night,

there should burst with shouts and torches the monstrous
and obscene band of a Callot orgy. What unbelievable
forces urging her towards a share in real life, beyond the
round of shop-gazing and the prattle of her likes, must
have been massing up behind the dam of her education
and reserve before such a meeting could take place! What
abominable science in this man of the unexplainable sufferings of a woman's heart before he could dare to sidle
up, cough, raise his hat, look at her eyes and begin to tell
her what he thought of the weather!

We need not resort to the absurd fable that Smith
completely deceived her. Truth loves economy; there is no
need to make her a fool, or him a genius. There is a simpler likelihood that he did not try to conceal his rank or
the (unspecified) badness of his past. The first would have
been useless in a country where a man cannot open his
mouth without betraying his breeding. The second, presented without details, might have been necessary as a
counterweight to the first. A proletarian such as Smith's
opening vowels must have announced, whose life had been
a humdrum, would neither have dared to accost Miss
Mundy, nor would she have carried the acquaintance farther. When she set out to see the evening alone; when she
noticed at the turning that a man was following her; and
after the first flurry slacked her pace, then stopped against
the railing and waited; when she saw him come near
with a swagger in his arms and hesitation in his feet, and
saw the soldier's shoulders and the shape of biceps in his
coat-sleeves, the carefully jutted chin, it was not expecta-
tion, be sure, of a talk with an industrious artisan

that made her breathing an embarrassing pleasure and prompted her little bow. It was a messenger who brought a ticket to life, the great ball of pain and change from which she had been lawfully but unjustly excluded; he must prove he had lived.

So, as soon as she could help him to it, the bold spectre must have declared that he had a wild past. They parted late, she to notice the change in her room, as if all the furniture had been moved and ornamented, from the black hygienic bedstead to the row of pocket poets in limp leather. He, to exercises of deductive arithmetic, working from half-perceived rings and a brooch to the unknown resources of ladies that *were* ladies. Sleep sound, both of you; don't worry that the other will not keep the rendezvous. Henceforth your lives, and your deaths, are welded together.

In two days they were kissing. In three they were off to Weymouth. No half-human plausibility could have seduced her at this speed. The population of fifty genteel boarding-houses had been pushing her to it for ten years. Her decision had been under steam for ten years; Smith's knuckles only needed to touch the throttle. Nor was it a mad flight; her companion's grudging of the marriage fees could not dissuade her from two rooms, the first night, and four days later a permission from the registrar to Henry Williams, thirty-five, bachelor, picture-restorer, son of Henry John Williams, commercial traveller, and Bessie Constance Mundy, to sleep as they pleased thereafter. She, indeed, not Life, had the last word in the bargain after all, and wrung her contract, in the exact prescribed terms of life-long support and faithfulness, out of the very jaws of the adventure. The same evening Smith was mollified for his expense and trouble by learning the value of his prize. Hereupon he sat down after supper and wrote to his bride's trustee recalling to him that £8 a month on £2,500 left odd shillings in hand, which in the course of years must now amount to no less than £138, for which he would be obliged to request early remittance, at your earliest possible convenience. A postscript in the hand of his niece informed the trustee both of her adventure and its triumphant success.

This stage is summed up by the lover himself, in his admirably personal style, in another letter to her trustee uncle.

14 RODWELL AVENUE, WEYMOUTH,
29th August 1910.

Dear Sir,

My wife and self thank you very much for your letter today with kind expressions. In *re* banks, undoubtedly to transact the business there would be rather awkward. Thus we suggest it would be better if you will be good enough to forward a money order instead of checks—however it will suit the circumstances. Any time we change our address we should let you know beforehand. Bessie hopes you will forward as much money as possible at your earliest (by registered letter). Am pleased to say Bessie is in perfect health, and both looking forward to a bright and happy future.

Believe me, yours faithfully,

H. WILLIAMS.

On this was added, in her hand: 'I am very happy indeed.—BESSIE WILLIAMS.'

This letter was the beginning of a month's postal struggle between the trustee and Smith, in which each called in the aid of solicitors. As for Bessie Williams, her will is asleep, either from the exhaustion of the upheaval, or because her uncle's goodwill, having been risked in the greater, did not count with her in the lesser injury her husband was doing to it. Meanwhile, the subject of his past was tacitly dropped between them, with the phraseology of courtship; indeed his romantic sins seemed to fade into nothing but a busy and painstaking greed for money. He was always absent-minded, always waiting for the post, or preparing another letter for it. The solicitor they visited together deposes that she sat silent at the interviews. She was probably puzzled, but inwardly convinced, since the marriage certificate was there, that in the end it would be all right.

The moment that the money came, at last, Smith had used all the time he had to spare for her. He cashed it in gold and disappeared. It was part of his terrible thrift that he never left a woman without writing back to her some vague excuse, as if to save her for an uncertain, unplanned future use. Although he had thoroughly convinced himself that there was not the dimmest possibility of touching through her the locked-up capital of her fortune, over which the raging uncle was mounting a fierce guard with all the power of the law on his side, yet the mysterious man did not neglect his usual leave-taking. But in this case, besides the disturbing recommendations to save money, more precise and more menacing than ever before—

> Ask your uncle about a week before the 8th to always
> send your cash in a money order so that you can change
> it at the P. O. Pay the landlady 25s. weekly for board
> and lodging and take my advice and put 30s. out of the
> £8 into the Savings Bank—so it will come handy for
> illness or other emergencies or for us when I return. If
> you do not I shall be angry when I return—

—there was a new and dreadful variation in the pretext
for the desertion. In his flights from other women, Smith
had never gone beyond a vague plea of 'urgent business.'
But to this poor devil he made a charge (that she had
infected him with venereal disease) that showed a bloody
hatred, already full grown. We are now at last treading
near that lust of killing, that apparition from the depths,
whose fullest meaning will appear in the case of Haarmann. Such an insult, unnecessary as well as untrue,
could not be an accident tacked on to the hurried lie of a
coarse rogue. It is an act, a corporal violence, like the
thong of a whip laid across her face, the apparently senseless, but by no means causeless, worrying of a sheep by a
vicious dog. The passivity, the meekness of this educated
woman had aroused some other nameless devil in him beside his biting fear-born avarice. Other dupes were to him
only jumping figures in a cash-book. This most unhappy
woman was to him flesh and blood. She had landed on
the island of his egotism; he was afraid he was not alone.

Shaking off her presence with the blow he went back
to his realities, the pasteboard wife he had contrived for
himself, the mortgages and the deeds. A week after his
sin, he was in the office of the Insurance Company, with
a bag of sovereigns, asking to pay off £93 of the mortgage.
He began to play at dealing again, and took Miss Pegler-

Smith to Southend, then Walthamstow, then Barking Road, London, then back to Bristol again, his fort. For two years he seems to have lived without another victim. The Mundy episode had scared him—without any obvious cause, for even a novice would know that he would never hear from her again.

She showed the letter to her landlady; then when she was able to travel her brother came and fetched her away.

In February 1912, Smith had no more money. The presentiment, or whatever it was, fatigue or inertia, that had kept him in his own quarters for two years, notwithstanding, must be thrown off and another slinking adventure begun. He handed over the bare shop to his creature (she sold the goodwill for £5) and he disappeared again. She watched his train out of sight 'steaming in an easterly direction,' and then packed up and returned to her mother's. Another of Smith's hoards put away neatly until wanted.

On the 14th of March in the same year, Bessie 'Williams' is a guest at the house of Mrs. Tuckett, a boarding-house called 'Norwood' at Weston-super-Mare. Mrs. Tuckett knows what is the matter with her, for Bessie's aunt has told her the story. She is always called Miss Mundy. She is treated with firm kindness, as if she was an invalid; sent out for a walk at regular hours; encouraged to eat a lot. On this day she went out at eleven to do a small commission for Mrs. Tuckett. She returned late, at past one o'clock, 'very excited.' As soon as she had gone out she had met her husband. He was looking over the sea; she went up and touched him. He turned round and said: 'All a mistake.' Mrs. Tuckett listened to this with

pressed lips and sent a wire with the news of the catastrophe to Miss Mundy's aunt. At three o'clock the man
himself arrived, unendingly loquacious. While he was talking, Mrs. Tuckett sat still and stiff; Bessie, in her chair,
thinking of something else. When his spring grew sluggish,
Mrs. Tuckett asked him, hard and dry, why he had left
his wife at Weymouth? He replied with a new gush, sideways, that he had been looking for her for twelve months,
'in every town in England.' Mrs. Tuckett said that she did
not understand the necessity, seeing that he knew the address of her relations. He answered quickly that, as a matter of fact, it was her brother or her uncle who had finally
put him on the track.

He lied. The meeting on the front, however it might
seem to show traces of human handiwork, was the freak
product of nature, or Destiny, who had arranged her cos-
mic timetables to suit, to ruin this pair. One of them, possibly both, did not desire the meeting, before it was
malevolently thrust upon them by Providence. But, now it
was accomplished, neither would call the bluff of the Gods
and fly for their lives. Each reaccepted the other as food
for that hungry imagination; each lived marooned with a
character to be woven into the story each was living;
Bessie had her human, handsome man again to be re-
formed, submitted to; Smith recovered a good business
project to be carried to success by strict attention and dili-
gence. That very afternoon he took her to a solicitor,
signed a note acknowledging a 'loan' of the £150 with
interest at 4 per cent. It was his idea of perfect reconcilia-
tion. Hers was to sit still and nod to all this queer simple
lover proposed. In the enthusiasm of a man who returns

from a long holiday, Smith turned to arrears of work and with the same candid methods as before tried his best to reconcile the family. An ordinary explanation might be difficult, but could they resist the straight thing from a solicitor? So his version of the return went to the uncle and brother, emphatically adorned with mention of the 4 per cent., under the stamped heading and over the signature of Messrs. Baker & Co., solicitors. But Smith's veneration of the law and all the actions of its limbs is not necessarily shared by honest men. His stamped and witnessed excuses only alarmed the relatives.

That night Bessie said to Mrs. Tuckett: 'I suppose I may go back to my husband?' The good woman, angry but helpless, replied: 'You are over thirty, I cannot hold you back.' Man and wife they went away, promising to come back that night, but did not return. Instead, Smith sent a letter which did more credit to his reformatory teachers of what was the 'right thing' than his picked-up superstition about solicitors' letters. In it is, in solution, the whole of his views on the British middle-class, their ethics, their customs and their numerous soft spots. It must be read in full.

> Weston-super-Mare 15. 3. 12.
> Dear Madam—In consequence of the past and the heated argument which possibly would have occurred if wife and self had to face you and your friends this evening, thus, for the sake of peace we decided to stop away and remain together as man and wife should do in the apartments which I have chosen temporarily. Later on I will write a long letter to all Bessie's friends clearly puporting all the circumstances of the whole affair solely with the intention of placing all your minds at rest concerning our welfare. All I propose to state at present

beside that which has already been stated by Bessie and
myself before the solicitors that it is useless as the law
stands and in view of all the circumstances together with
the affinity existing between my wife and self for any
person to try and part us and dangerous to try and do us
harm or endeavour to make our lives miserable. It appears
that many people would rather stir up strife than try and
make peace. As far as Bessie and I are concerned the past
is forgiven and forgotten. Bessie has not only stated that
on her oath to the solicitors; but has also given it out to
me in a letter written by herself to me which I shall always prize. Thus my future object and delight will be to
prove myself not only a true husband but a gentleman
and finally make my peace step by step with all those
who have been kind to Bessie. Then why in the name of
heaven and Christianity do people so like to constantly
interfere and stir up past troubles. It would be more
christian like and honourable on their part to do their
best to make peace. There is time yet to make amends
and if people will only let us alone and with the help of
the higher powers which has united us twice, Bessie shall
have a comfortable settled home and be happy with me.
I trust there is many many years of happiness before us.
I thank with all my heart all those who have been kind
to my wife during my absence.

Yours respectfully,

H. WILLIAMS.

In this witness to the influence of the three pillars of
Smith-society on Smith's soul, the parson, the magistrate, and the solicitor, it is only needful to comment that
the cautious threat, without which hardly any letter of the
man is complete, would not imply any physical reprisal,
but only to bring the law on them. Pleased with this effort
and still full of zeal, Smith went on to write another to
the brother, which begins with the peerless lines: *Dear
Sir—I know not how I shall offend in dedicating my un-*

polished lines to you nor how you will censure me for using so strong a prop for supporting so grave a burden. . . . To this Bessie had added a postscript—her correspondence from the moment of the reunion was all at the tail of her husband's screeds—in which was the terrible phrase heavy with all the besotted illusions of her whole life: '*I know my husband better now than ever before. I am perfectly happy.*'

Meanwhile the incubus, gravely satisfied with the 'steps' he had taken, now devoted himself to a long examination of that trust-fund. Before making any definite plans on it he consulted the supreme oracle of his world: counsel's opinion, which made it clear that the mutual wills he had devised were useless, and that the only way to be certain of laying hands on it was that its owner should die, quickly, before the trustees, set on 'stirring up strife and unpleasantness,' exercised their power of using it to buy an annuity for her. Those sinister 'higher powers' were closing in on Smith now, like policemen, to march him to that bourn in which he and Bessie will never again come upon each other by accident.

They were now at Herne Bay. In this climax, in which he would show all that he was, all that he had grown to, all that he had been taught, Smith will not desert the wide sands where he was most at ease. On May 20th he hires a house in the High Street. To the clerk of the owner, Miss Rapley (afterwards an important witness against him), he is talkative and conciliatory: 'My wife is a cut above me,' he confides to Miss Rapley. 'Her friends did not at all approve of her marriage. My wife has a private income paid monthly. I have not anything except that; I dabble in antiques.' At the end of his confidences, he was allowed to pay in advance for the rent instead of producing banker's references. The house, one suspects, must have been hard to let, possibly because of the old-fashioned absence of a bath, or he would not have been accepted as a tenant, for he made a doubtful impression on shrewd Miss Rapley.

Mutual wills were drawn up and executed on July 8th. The next day Smith went to the shop of Hill, ironmonger, and bargained for a tin bath. £2 was the price asked. He got it for £1 17s. 6d. It had no taps or fittings, but had to be filled and emptied with a bucket.

One more thing remains, before the end. On the day following Smith took Bessie to a young doctor, and stated to him that she had had some sort of a fit the previous day, and had lost consciousness. It is most probable that Smith meant a 'fainting fit,' which may or may not have had some foundation in fact. The doctor decided that he meant an epileptic fit; passed him leading questions on the symptoms, to which Smith agreed. This lesson on epilepsy Smith retained for future use. The woman did not remember anything so serious having happened to her; she had always been healthy; since Mr. Williams said so, it must have come and gone outside her consciousness. All that she remembered was a headache. With a prescription for bromide of potassium they went home.

The next night, past midnight, Smith returned to the surgery and rang the night-bell. His wife had had another fit: please to come at once. When the two men reached the bedroom, Mrs. Williams was sitting up, hot and flushed. It was a Senegalian night; she complained of the heat. At three next afternoon Smith and she went again to the dispensary; she looked in perfect health. Smith said she was much better. That same night she wrote to her uncle: 'Last Tuesday night I had a bad fit. . . . My whole system is shaken. My husband has provided me with the best medical men, who are . . . attending me day and night. I have made my will and left all to my husband. That is only natural as I love my husband. . . .'

This letter can only mean that the romantic obedience she was playing at had ended in her quite laying aside the use of her brain: a perilous thing for any human being, in any circumstances. Reason, sublime and faithful ally in all the snares with which our life is so beset, is never to be jilted, even for Love, even for Piety, even for that fidgety gossip, Conscience—who indeed had nothing to say to this poor woman dreaming with all her might, on the brink of the gulf. Nor was the killer himself, in these last days, better guided. As completely as his victim he had abandoned good sense. In its place he was plying himself with all the mental drugs to which his miserable life had made him addict, soaking himself with illusions, to tone his will for the infernal leap just ahead. Until now he had practised only sharp dealing, of a size and shape indeed that society particularly despises, but still possible for the trained imagination of a prison-formed egotist to accept as equally meriting the name 'business' as company-promotion or munition-manufacture. But now he had come to a profound verge where ordinary self-deception must fail, to a limit over which, if ever he was to sleep again, he must be aided by a wilder, stronger illusion. To the making of this hypnosis in the few days that remain, he intensifies all his ways of thinking, as an athlete prepares his muscles for a record test. Everything that could recall to him the Reality, the personality of the woman beside him, he rigidly put out of mind. At all costs he must regard her as 'raw material,' and crush out every reminder of her humanity. To this end he calls in the aid of every drop of disgust and contempt which in his nature of *faux-homme-aux-femmes* he felt for all women but one. For fear she should 'put him under an obligation' he insists on doing all the housework himself, this lazy man. He does the shopping and insists on her staying in bed late, so that he can hate her. He had all the mean tidiness of routine of the incipient miser, he encouraged a hundred daily irritations of it; and he carefully concealed from her the way he liked things done, so that she could offend him. For the last few days he even paid the bills out of his own pocket, though every day he got nearer his last penny. The ways of a murderer and a boa-constrictor are opposite. Where the one sweetens with his saliva, the other must carefully contrive to hate. To the same end, he refused to listen to any account of her life since they parted, pretexting his sensitive remorse; he definitely cut her strand by strand from life in his mind and memory before he killed her. Above all, he insisted with himself that it was business, business; and for this he forced himself to think only on the ledger-side of what he was doing. For this he haggled over the bath; if for the first time in his life he had bought a second-hand object without huckstering it would have been to recognize to himself that this was not business, but murder. In the nights he called up the ethics they had taught him, clause by clause; the pettifogging religion of the police-courts, the casuistry of evidence, that makes or unmakes a crime; and cited to himself many social examples of crimes that were not crimes; recalled from his soldier days that killing need be no murder. So with nourishing of contempt, watering of hatred, with artificial incomprehension, with the exercise of his life-system of thought, he diligently prepared himself to kill. If he had more difficulty than those whose cases we have examined before, it may be an illusion due to our lack of knowledge, unjustly favouring him or depreciating his breed-mates; it may be that this man, the most odious of all mass-murderers, in reality had less aptitude for the trade than the rest.

Then on Saturday morning, so that the inquest could pass without her relatives being able to hear the news and attend (owing to the absence of Sunday mails), he calls his wife at seven o'clock and suggests to her she should take a bath. There was a reason apparently why this should be not opportune; but intent on her Griselda-play she obeys. He had placed the bath, not in its natural place —an empty room over the kitchen where there was but one flight of stairs to mount with the water-buckets—but in another room, a flight farther: because the kitchen room had a bolt, the other, none.

At eight o'clock the same doctor as before, summoned by a note, enters the house, is met by Williams, and taken to the bathroom. In it, cold and naked, lies Bessie Mundy, drowned. A square piece of Castile soap was clutched in her right hand. Williams was calm and very ready with her dates and hours. Another who had found murder

easier than he expected! His story was that he had gone
out to fetch herrings for breakfast; when he returned his
wife was dead. With this story the coroner, in spite of a
letter of cautious warning from the brother, and his jury
agreed. Smith's behaviour must now carefully be watched;
there is much to learn from it. He has two problems, one
inward—the struggle with himself, to keep his nerves
straight and his heart on ice; the other objective—to carry
out his simple plot to delude the police. The second is
obviously the easier. He has only to stick to his pat story
of the earlier visits to the doctor and point resignedly to
the bath. But even so there are flaws in it, bad flaws,
which in the presence of the letter from Herbert Mundy
the coroner must have been uncommonly dense not to
see. Why did Smith not lift her at once out of the water?
Why did he wait for the doctor to find her with her face
submerged? Why should the bath be placed in an in-
convenient room without a lock? And especially, how
could a woman of her stature be drowned, unaided, in a
bath too small for her? The plan over which some have
wasted intellectual admiration was only the elementary
cunning of a second-rate mind; with any intelligence to
contend with, Smith would have ended his career of murderer at his first kill. His inward problem too has a nasty
repercussion. He is in the quandary: I dare not feel any pity
for her: how am I to show it? Show it he ought to, and here
he is a failure. The clerk of the landlord, Miss Rapley, related later Smith's awful complaisance; in her presence he
made a bad pretence of weeping and talked about the
'lucky thing my wife had made her will.' Every one he
had to relate the happening to had the same impression:

the woman who came to lay out the body, who found it lying naked on the bare boards; the undertaker, whom Smith instructed to bury his wife in a common grave, in the cheapest manner possible; the relations, to whom again he sent grossly unconvincing letters, packed with sentences such as 'Words cannot describe the great shock, and I am naturally too sad to write more': enough to rouse the suspicions of a Bessie Mundy herself. But Smith is caught in his own gin, from which neither here nor in later murders can he shake free; he has set his mind to think his victims into business items. Without this he could not have done away with them, and it is impossible to feign without trying to feel. For this reason he is obliged to keep the money advantage of her death so constantly in his mind that it slips out to Miss Rapley; for this reason he is obliged to huckster the very coffin; for this reason he cannot squeeze out even one sympathetic word to her relations; for this reason he is obliged to plunge at once into the most cold-blooded and suspicious attempts to collect her fortune. The family entered a caveat against the will; but later, discouraged by the coroner's verdict, and secretly afraid of the fellow snarling at the bottom of the affair, they yielded and Smith received the wage of his damnation. The day after, 'Williams' had vanished, and Smith was writing to his institutional wife, Edith Pegler, to join him in Margate. She told him she had searched for him everywhere, even calling at his accommodation address with the Insurance Company at Woolwich. At this he made as if he would strike her with his fist, then suddenly thinking of something else, contented himself with a warning never again to try to look into his affairs. He told her

he had been to Canada again, done big business with a
Chinese idol picked up for a song and sold for over
£1,000, and went to write business letters.

With the money, the tormented man now began an
intricate and fundamentally idiotic series of transactions,
transferring his money (split up in innumerable cheques)
from one bank and from one end of the country to the
other, as if he was afraid it would melt away, or be traced;
really, to beguile his mind by the pretence of constant
business. When he was tired of this form of the game of
Patience, he embarked on an equally miscellaneous series
of property transactions, an orgy of buying and selling,
signing and releasing, and entering and transferring, which
lasted for months, dealt with some ten small houses and
ended, as far as an outsider in such matters can judge,
with a net loss of over £700. Another idea then seized
him—its origin is sufficiently obvious—he would have no
more houses, but an annuity, that brought money in regularly. On this he spent what remained of the woman's
money, to bring in £76 1*s*. a year. Then some time later,
he thought better of it, and tried to release the money
again for some other series of operations he had thought
out, but after its wild excitements the fortune of Bessie
Mundy had reached immobility. The purchase of an an-
nunity cannot be repented.

To the agent who had sold him this annuity (Mr.
Plaisance), Smith, in October 1913, brought new business, and at the same time made an enigmatic promise to
buy another £500 worth of annuity 'out of land transactions in Canada,' the following January. For this business
he was obliged to return to his real name, and even to

forgo all mythology and produce his birth certificate. So the next episode, his marriage with Alice Burnham, is played out in the name of Smith. It was this young woman, a stout merry nurse, in the best of health and spirits, whose life Smith insured with Plaisance. At first Smith wanted the sum to be £1,000, payable at death; but learning that marriage would make the premium on this amount out of his means, he contented himself with one for £500 on a twenty-year endowment.

· His confidence in the 'Canadian' deal shows that he had fully made up his mind to continue in the trade for which Bessie Mundy had paid his apprenticeship. That, to make it pay, he was resolved to turn to the most common and dangerous method of life-insurance, which has hanged innumerable murderers before him. The exploitation of death ranges from the horrible sale of the body itself, as with Burke (but there are even simpler means than that, as we shall see in the case of Haarmann), which solves the problem of disposal of the body and covers its tell-tale witness to the cause of death; through the simple despoliation of the personal possessions of the victim—furniture in the case of Landru, trust funds in the example of Bessie Mundy—to the insurance fraud, which Smith was now premeditating. There is no other method to gain money by the death of a person who has no possessions, and Smith was, for whatever reason, unable to venture on another moneyed spinster. But the essence of mass-murder, to be profitable and safe, is that the victims must stand in a loosened relation to the rest of society. The wolf who knows his business only attacks the isolated members of the herds, the wanderers, the outliers. To strict observance of this principle, Burke owed his immunity. It was in a terrific attempt to snap the chains that bound Kinck to his fellow-men that Troppmann peopled the plain of Pantin with corpses. But the exploitation of life-insurance, while it allows on the one hand of the selection of poor strayers —riches being the most powerful chain to hold society's interest in a man's personal fate—yet the very act of giving a powerful commercial organization a direct interest that the victim should not die wakens an enemy whose determination and acumen is more dangerous to the assassin than all the Dogberrys of all the local inquest courts. Thus, while apparently cunning, it is the stupidest folly for a professional murderer to pick out a friendless victim and then give the victim's life over to the protection of a most powerful and interested corporation. It is a common folly, and tempted that stupid rogue, Smith. Nor indeed was his intended victim, this Alice Burnham, without friends. Her father was a retired coal-merchant, immensely more shrewd than the small shyster that thus pushed into his family circle; there were brothers, sisters, and a mother who loved her. Only over the girl herself, whom he had met in his accustomed manner at Portsmouth, had the murderer any advantage; not one, to be sure, of intellect, but given to him, an eligible male, by nature and the social system. Miss Burnham is a less enigmatic character than her predecessor, though hardly less tragic. She was a strong capable woman, hard-working in her profession, to whom celibacy with all its accompaniments was as irksome as it was despairing to Bessie Mundy. Every atom of Miss Burnham's body and her tastes repelled her from the state to which the customs of her country had condemned her.

She was twenty-six years old when she accepted the company of this man, of whom she could have had less illusions even than Bessie. She was eager to risk all the smug-faced monotony of comfort and esteem, even the affection of her family, for the single chance of a natural life; and she was a cheerful gambler.

But first she made a bold attempt to impose her 'young man' (Smith was now 40) on her family. Smith cut a pitiable figure at the family home in Aston Clinton, where he was invited; the bluff father had met many such before, and concealed neither his contempt nor dislike for this stranger whose manner wavered always between brag and servility. The mother, whose ideas of the minimum qualifications of a husband were less exacting than those of Charles Burnham, tried to moderate her husband; but in the end the prospective son-in-law was kicked out, muttering threats, and Alice accompanied him to the station. That was the 31st October 1913. On the 4th November following they were married, without anyone of the family being present.

On retiring from business, Mr. Burnham had presented each of his children with £40, the eldest son taking over the succession. To this sum Alice, from her savings, had added £60, and given the whole £100 to her father for safe keeping. He paid her 4 per cent on it. This nest-egg Smith now set himself to collect, with his mixture of greed and legal stupidities. He poured forth a stream of letters to the father in his usual county-court cum lay-reader tone; he accused him of 'taking refuge in obdurateness, contempt, and remorse,' and threatened 'to take the matter up without delay.' In the course of the correspondence, a post-card from Smith conveyed the genealogical information at the beginning of this study. Another ran, 'I do not know your next move, but take my advice and be careful.' Another pointed this vague threat (with sounds nastier to us who know the man's past than probably it was intended) with the explanation, 'I am keeping all letters that pass for the purpose of justice.' In the end, Burnham, dreading a long and vexatious law-case with this sinister sea-lawyer, yielded and sent the money.

By this ungainly procedure, Smith had achieved the opposite of what he no doubt intended, and set an estrangement between the daughter and her family. A similar action about a paltry sum owed by her sister completed the effect. But without meaning it, he had blundered into the only possible chance of the success of the deed he was planning—the isolation of the woman. The next act in his fixed repertory which he had composed from the circumstance of his first crime, after the habit of mass-murderers, was to take Alice Burnham on a trip to Blackpool. In the choice of this distant resort, he showed both a knowledge of geography and a nice science of the social usages. Blackpool in winter is out of season, yet the relaxation of censure and curiosity still might be hoped to prevail. The respectable by-roads of Herne Bay suited admirably in his former venture; but both the life and death of the gay little nurse would fit better into the setting of the People's Paradise of the North. And it was as far as possible from her family and any friends her infatuation for him could have left.

When they arrived in the cold grey air, there were no tunes from the merry-go-rounds to greet them, the shoot-ing-galleries were quiet; the promenade empty and windy. They put up for their unseasonal honeymoon with a family named Crossley, in lodgings in Cocker Street. Previously Smith had tried elsewhere, but failed to find the convenience of a bathroom. In the Crossleys' house, for ten shillings a week, they could use the bath when they liked. All they had brought for luggage was a brownish holdall and a paper parcel. The Crossleys were good Lancashire folk, very anxious to please in this lodgerless month. Mrs. Crossley agreed to cook the visitors' meals. They would buy the materials themselves. Smith knows no other method of preparing himself for great acts than to soak his mind in petty meannesses. He grumbles astonishingly at the departure of every penny. Mrs. Smith seemed to the Crossleys charming; it is a pity that this Mrs. Smith has a train-headache from the journey. But in spite of it and Mr. Smith's already noticeable stinginess, she insists on going out the same evening to the kinematograph.

Smith is desperately quick this time; he is afraid this lively little Alice will either escape him or ruin him. Nevertheless he does not scamp a detail of his plaster-of-Paris plan. The morning after their arrival, he takes her to the doctor; naturally this time does not dare to talk of fits (she is a nurse), but insists that the railway-headache alarms him. The doctor is not at a loss: he prescribes a mild purgative.

Two days later, that was a Friday, they went out for a walk, leaving instructions for a bath to be prepared. The bath was to be for Mrs. Smith. Smith had already inspected the bathroom. Before this look-round the bolt worked perfectly. It was above the kitchen. At tea-time, the evening meal, the Crossleys, the mother, the son, the grown-up daughter-in-law, were sitting round the kitchen table, when one of them noticed a great stain of water on the ceiling. They all looked at it and saw it enlarge and drip down the wall, behind a picture. Such a thing had never happened before. The elder woman said, 'Oh, Alice, go and tell Mrs. Smith not to fill the bath so.' But the girl answered, 'Oh, mother, they will think we are grumbling already, and they not two days in the house.'

Then suddenly the pale Smith came into the kitchen. He lumped a package on to the table and said, 'I have brought these eggs for our breakfast in the morning.' The girl got up to take them, wiping her mouth with her napkin. Smith then went upstairs. They heard him call shrilly, 'Alice, put the light out.' The daughter-in-law, who had this Christian name, thought he was speaking to her, rose and went up to him. He said, 'No, I was speaking to my wife, Alice, to put the light out.' The living Alice went back into the kitchen. Then Smith, who was standing on the mat on the bathroom landing, said suddenly again, 'My wife will not speak to me.' Good Mrs. Crossley stood up at this sort of scream, and said, 'Oh, what is it?' 'Fetch Dr. Billing in a hurry,' he said.

Mrs. Crossley: Dr. Billing lives quite near. I ran for him and he came to my house for a few minutes. I waited on the stairs and when he came down I asked him what was wrong, and he said, 'Oh, she is drowned. She is dead.' Smith was upstairs on the landing then. I went back to the kitchen and my daughter, called Mrs. Haynes, came in. After the doctor had gone, Smith came down into the kitchen. I said to him, 'How dreadful: what an awful thing this is!' He said he would not be surprised at anything that would happen afterwards.

Behind this stiffness that shocked we may catch a glimpse of a soul clinging with all its might to unreality, a wretch, terror-stricken to the heart, striving with all his might to believe that he had simply done a good stroke of business. Under the water-splash on the ceiling, amidst the remnant of an evening meal, the two eyed each other, he helpless to relax his grip, not daring even to pretend to cry, she with an angry uneasiness growing every second. They are both tongue-tied. She breaks it off finally, in a new tone. 'Now, Smith, you cannot stop here to-night.' He can only say, 'Why?' 'Because I'll take good care not to have a callous fellow like you in the house.' He gulps, but does not protest, except, 'When they're dead, they're dead.' He had to write his letters in the next-door house that night. Across the post-card on which he left with her his address, Mrs. Crossley wrote, in spite of the inquest, in spite of the verdict, the memento, 'Wife died in bath. We shall see him again.'

This bungler had succeeded again. The mere fact that the woman had died in a bath and that no one as yet had heard of this stealthy form of murder seemed alone to be in his favour. Hangdog and perpetually busy, he fixed his affairs, collected the money from the company without a murmur, and paid over to Plaisance the promised £500. Acting more near instinct than by free thought he repeated the chain of his acts as he had devised them in the former case, down to their least detail. He had prepared the doctor, prepared her parents, killed on Friday to avoid their

presence, made up the same trumpery alibi of a small purchase outside. Now he completed the chain, sold the dead
woman's jewels and clothing and cleared out to another
sea-town, then sent for the Bristol wife, with another tale
of dealings in Canada.

The success of this second murder must have confirmed the man in the complicated unreality he had adjusted round himself. He no longer found it hard to
believe that he was a bold business man, successful in a
very serious line, who must, after all, look after his health.
He became exacting with Pegler; with those annuities
locked in his private drawer, he dared to begin to believe
he had done it 'all for her.' The thought of another long
sea-voyage to Canada, to find another valuable antique,
oppressed him more than it did his companion; he had
made symbols like this for everything in his life and used
them even in his private thoughts. Every day he seemed
more cynical about the hardness of the world. He pitied
himself profoundly, because his nature was a handicap.
He confided to his wife sometimes parts of what he had
suffered in his last journey: how a certain man had tried to
humiliate him about his birth, how the miserable suspicions of boarding-house keepers and the like just showed
you. So by these symbolisms he managed to relieve himself of the only burden that weighed, the memory of hu-
miliations, the scratches on his pride. Then he would
spend hours reading the small print on the backs of his
annuities and checking his old house-accounts. At intervals he would be stung with the recollection of what he had
lost and he would leave the Bristol house for a week's trip.

But never as far as Canada—lesser affairs in the earlier manner. Matters of savings, small deals with servants and the like.

At last those higher powers, who had so whimsically rejoined him and Bessie together, again intervened. At Clifton, near the spot where a man he knew named Henry Williams once met a girl called Mundy, he fell in with Miss Margaret Lofty, a small, wistful shape, who was walking in the cool of the evening to calm certain private anguishes. She was the daughter of a clergyman, dead for years, a lady's companion no longer young. A year before, she had been happy, but the man she was engaged to had turned out a married man and now she was alone. She was struck by Smith's eyes, eyes that showed he too had suffered, eyes that gave her the sensation of 'having been there before.' She learned that his name was 'Lloyd,' a man beneath her station, of course, but a God-fearing, handsome fellow who understood.

She clung to him as if she were drowning. She made a show for him of all her accomplishments, fell in eagerly with all his ideas. When he talked about insurance and how it was a principle of his to make provision for the future, she picked up all its mechanism in an hour or two's quiet chat. He complimented her on her intelligence, regretted he had not had himself the advantage of much education. A shy and retiring man; he was too nervous to meet her family, which suited her, as she felt a tiny grudge against her mother and sister for their uncomprehension in the terrible affair the year before, and now they might not understand. At thirty-eight a woman's affairs are her own concern, and seldom easy to tell. She told them nothing about Lloyd, and made up an innocent story about a new position (which was true after all) when she went away to be married. After she had gone to see the insurance-manager (she struck him as 'having the business at her finger's ends') and taken out a policy for £700, 'Lloyd' had the license ready. They took train to Bath and the same day were man and wife.

Miss Lofty drew out her life savings, £19, and advanced it to her husband. This money carried them to London, where Smith, who knew the neighbourhood from one of his former existences, had booked lodgings in the superior district of Highgate. Coroner's juries would push complaisance to its limits in such a neighbourhood. But when they arrived at the address, Smith-Lloyd had a great shock. He stumbled across the war.

For during all these years while the man intent in his own cult pursued his private ritual of murder, a mightier killing was being prepared, a world-wide massacre, one of whose immense circuits of force lay through the very house he had selected for his last crime. As absent-minded as a weasel on the blood-scent, possibly until this moment he had never heard of the war. It was the 17th December 1914, the miraculous year. The day before, his own hunting-grounds, Scarborough, Whitby, were shelled by German cruisers. Two months before the London mob in a patriotic ecstasy had sacked the German shops, and every unfortunate German in the country was still trembling. Amongst them the mistress of the very house that he had chosen. On his first visit he had noticed her attitude. Little in a woman's manner ever escaped that professional eye. So automatically he had swelled in *his* manner, played the masterful. When she asked timidly for references, he did not give her an easy lie, but pulled six shillings out of his pocket and tapped them on the desk. She was afraid to refuse them; but more afraid, in such times, when every one of her actions was dangerous, to step even for an inch outside the safety of law. When he returned with the woman, this foreign woman had fortified herself with a supreme reinforcement, a real detective, friend of the family. It was this man (Dennison) who met the couple when they arrived and told Smith-Lloyd, with one of those precognitional glances of which those of his calling have the secret, to be off, and quickly.

The couple went out in silence, at hazard, when Smith had been paid his deposit. In a side-road near by, Bismarck Road, they found another place, kept by Miss Blatch. His formula, for a moment checked, begins to run: 'Have you a bath?' They are accepted. Then Mrs. Lloyd sits down to send the letter mentioning an illness; then they visit the nearest doctor, then the preparation of the bath, and the full canon of the slaying; with this exception, that there was a splash, a sigh, a strange visit of the man to the harmonium where he played 'something' for a few minutes. Mrs. Lloyd is dead. There is again the rushing through the house, the terror of the landlady, the calls, the doctor's dash upstairs, the splashing in the bathroom, the policeman's knock on the door; evidence; a grim man who has a clear story and a bad manner, a word-for-word repetition in the coroner's court. Letters, packings, bargainings with grave-diggers, another £700 safely received.

But this time something more. A coincidence, one of those queer logical figures with which the stream of becoming sometimes playfully diversifies its course, one of life's punning rhymes, which science hates and art abhors, but which fascinate the attention of mankind. Smith, painstaking imitator of nature, who had modelled his ferocity on her accidents, had unthinkingly composed a perfect, a triple coincidence. He had been betrayed by the first law of murder: repetition. Let but one man stumble upon this coincidence of the bath and Smith by it alone, like an incurable poison, will die as surely and cruelly as Bessie Mundy.

That man was Charles Burnham. He noticed an account of the Highgate inquest in a Sunday newspaper, the *News of the World,* which is a collection of the happenings of the week, curious, dramatic, horrible and comic, immensely diffused among the English masses. 'Death' and 'Bride,' are index-words to the tastes of the readers of this journal; their conjunction in one case gave the news a good place in the paper. Almost with greed, this quiet unhurrying man, lying in not hopeless ambush for the return of the phantom who had destroyed his daughter, caught the devilish assonance, the infernal rhyme with all the circumstances of his own loss. The description of this Highgate mystery made Burnham's long-awaited revenge as simple then as the pull of a trigger; he cut out the printed account, pinned it to that in his possession of his own daughter's end, and sent them both to the police.

Thereafter there are two feverish activities running side

by side, one out of sight and below the other. The figure
of a man grown greyish, with an intangible history, working at accounts, very intent on the business of settling his
wife's affairs with solicitor, Somerset House, the Insurance
Company; and below him, like hounds out of sight in a
sunken road, the detectives grappling with his faint and
twisted trail back into the past. All that Smith may have
noticed in this fortnight is a slight clogging of his affairs,
an almost imperceptible increase of the customary delays,
the shadow of obscure inhibitions behind the Insurance
Company's formal letters. All his senses were sharpened
in the darkness in which he worked. At times, deep in his
correspondence, he would pause and listen as if through
their typed formalities he could hear a far-off noise of running steps. Sometimes for two days in succession he would
stop on his way to the solicitor's office and turn back
thoughtfully; then for long hours fight with himself to
pull back to the *business standpoint*. On the 1st of February 1915, as he left the solicitor's office, he saw with a
great start that three soberly dressed men wanted to speak
to him. They came round him so close that he felt their
coats, and one said something about Alice Burnham. As
in an accident, it was too sudden for him to have any fear.
If he had heard 'Miss Mundy' he might have screamed;
but the man said, 'Alice Burnham,' a name that only recalled a long and nasty business affair, in which he was in
the right, quite in the right, and no jury would give a verdict against him. So, without any blink he admitted that
he did know her, that he was the George Smith who had
married her at the Portsmouth Registry Office; what about
it? He was arrested at once on a charge of causing a false

entry in the marriage register. He did not need the customary caution not to say more.

England found time to try the man at the Old Bailey; for the nine days between 22nd June 1915, and the 1st July his affairs competed for public interest with the first defeats of the Russians in Galicia and the first victories of the Italians in the Dolomites. A prosy judge, a high spirited defender (Marshall Hall), let out the regulated driblets of information allowed by English law on the surly, absent-minded mystery fenced in their midst in dock. Under the weight of contrasts, Smith's deeds seemed more terrible than the crash of armies, his tin baths more evil things than bridge-destroying artillery, this minor devil more sinister than all the hell outside.

At times he would take his own part and yell at them. The whole court would stare at him with amazement as if his chop-law was speaking with tongues, and his blind belief in his own innocence—because they could not tell him the precise method he had killed, whether by pulling the feet, or by holding the heads—a thing never heard of in experience. But to this, and other last consolations of the mass-murderer, the inanimation of his victims, all trace of whose living personalities had long been expelled from his brain; the joy in the legal bickerings, so much to his taste; the sense of consideration and elevation that the dock confers—Smith, like Burke, like Troppmann, now felt himself entire. Alone in the court he neglected to look at the iron coincidence, three women identically killed, for identical motives after marriage with the same man, and attached importance to the cunning details which that recurrence contemptuously destroyed. Alone in the court, like a rigid juryman, he refused to believe in his own guilt, because a coincidence was not evidence.

These fundamental errors of thought no doubt sustained him in the condemned cell in which, a safe for precious objects, he was carefully preserved for death by hanging. Irreality has lordly rewards for her devotees, whether solipsists or drug fiends or murderers. In her humblest, more eerie form which had rotted this mass-murderer's imagination, she stood staunch by Smith to his end; if on the scaffold, with the ropes round his elbows and a bag over his mouth, his legs failed, it was a physical, not a moral terror that prevailed.

The
Poetry
of
Desiré
Landru

Avec la chute du jour, il me vient de sombres pensées. Aurions-nous terminé une chapitre du roman de Manon eternelle redite, et la belle page serait-elle lue jamais?

Letter from Landru (*signed L. Guillet*) written from Gambais to Fernande Segret.

THE LIFE AND DEATH OF GEORGE JOSEPH SMITH CONTAINS no doubt as many secrets as the Thames mud. It is a museum of the greeds and deformities of our times. But because of its peculiar air, lonely and base, it belongs a little too distinctly to one folk, one national form of society, and so, like much of our English imaginative creation, falls aside from universality. Smith, though all the characters of the trade of murder are in him, is too queerly shaped to be our typical mass-murderer. There are times with him that we feel a doubt whether we have plumbed the depths; whether he was really cut out for the business, or whether atrocity somehow has an arcanum so that there can be yet a more terrible thing than a murderer evolved by his fate; a man who forces himself to it with agonies of will; spiritual suicides as well as the providentially damned. No honest man can find trace of innocent madness in Smith. But there is a concentrated ugliness in his acts, an infernal snapping of teeth, even in his written words, that is supernaturally far worse than the romantic savageries of a Troppmann, or the gross terrors of a Burke, and appertains, we might fear to that higher power of evil in whom our fellow-countrymen have always been so curious. There are also accessory occasions or whims in Smith's life whose use we can hardly guess at—for example, why and what did he play on the American organ in the Highgate parlour? To dissolve this demoniac, local atmosphere of phantasy, and to shake out the general knacks of Smith's mind and method towards an elucidation of his fellow-agents of darkness, it is necessary to square him up beside one who, because he too was a killer of women for gain, has the same datum-line: Henri Desiré Landru.

By no means a simple operation; because this Landru, above all murderers in notoriety, is of them all the most tangled in the history of his boundless times; as if his personality, which was vastly more voluminous than that of any other criminal, adhered by its surface in infinite points to that society from which he was in 1919 violently ripped, opposite the tram-lines of Versailles. The differences in external characters between the man who confused the French nation's mind about the issue of the war, whose name was shouted in joke by tens of thousands along the whole line of the March of the Victors on 14th July, 1919; whose personality seems, to us who lived through them, to absorb or taint all the memories of the whirling Armistice months in Paris, when the potentates of the world were jerry-building a new era; in short, between the man who drove beards and Poiluism out of fashion among Frenchmen, and the haggard nonentity of Herne Bay, may well allow Landru to scorn the comparison. But with Landru the hobbyist, the waking dreamer, the technician in the forbidden trade, Smith, in spite of their nationalties, their variations in self-hallucination, their different *rank,* has strange things in common. With Landru, social phenomenon, more than a stare would discover, you will see it appear.

But first, around this case of Landru, explained by it, or at any rate commented, and quite necessary for its elementary understanding, is the concept of Landru's Paris. We must first have a social map of this endless tangle in which the strings of millions of individual human lives are knotted, which can only follow the lines of its industrial topography. For the space of a hundred miles' zone round the city are rich farming lands, split up into wedges of varying size by the radiation of the railway system. On these artificial routes runs, inwards, the current of foodstuffs to the central markets. Outwards to every segment of this agricultural circle there is a reflux of Parisians of all classes in the summer, to make the fortnight, month, or longer stay, which is the institution of *villégiature.* In this region, southward lies Gambais, where Landru rented his villa. Gambais differs in no other way from its sister-villages in the neighbourhood. The nice balance of their distance from the Colossus City has had uniformly two effects on their character. First their ancient quiet has been outwardly intensified. They have no permanent cinemas, few cafés, rare and rudimentary shops. With Paris within an hour's steam, who would want to shop or buy amusement for himself in Gambais? But all the noise of the world passes in the summer evenings through the main street, which sometimes is a roaring dust-flue containing a current of high-powered motor-cars that pass on their business.

Round this bed for the traffic stream, the village lies quite isolated; hundreds of concentric crooked streets, old and silent as the galleries of woodbeetles in a rafter. In the early morning cocks call across from one high wall to another. At noon dogs slumber undisturbed on the doorsills; in the first cool of the evening a hay-wain creaking with its weight turns down the alleys to its home-arch. With this subtly decadent stillness, Paris has stamped these thousand villages with another mark. They are materially more rustic than any other villages in France. But there is no gossip. Collective curiosity, corporate censure, is as dead there as their streets. For better or worse, the villages of the zone are discreet extensions of the residential quarters of the city, where there are no 'neighbours.' All round the mouldering nucleus of old houses in a Gambais where the peasant landlords sleep, is a thick crust of gimcrack, walled villas, each with its iron gate, its *cheval-de-frise* of broken glass, its hidden garden, where live the Parisians in fully-paid-for enjoyment of that capital city—luxury to which they are accustomed: privacy. The same unselective destiny as houses the Parisians in the great tenements at home, distributes them in their *villégiatures,* with no more discrimination or classification than a spade. Asmodeus could show off as varied a sight under the roofs of the villas of Gambais as in old Spain. An aged courtesan with a corrupt boy may share a party wall with a domesticated banker; a shy misanthrope who has survived a *cause célèbre* may walk in his garden and faintly hear on one side of him, out of sight next door, the laughs of a gay student and his grisette, on the other the daily scold-ings of a virtuous couple. Philosophers, artists and devils, fools, misers, or drug-eaters—all the infinite species of using out the span of fifty-four years insurance tables allot that men discover for themselves, may imaginatively be found among the summer tenants of Gambais in any year. It is probable (and the village gossips, having blunted their teeth years ago in the research, have come to that opinion) the majority of their city tenants are, like the rest of humanity, timid, rather dull people, to whom the prob-lem of money is the warp and woof of life. Among them, though, in the year 1918 was Henri Desiré Landru.

As the roads and rails through this root-zone of Paris converge, they seem physically to contract, and to concen-trate the look of the country. At a certain distance, the fields and pastures are squeezed into the allotments of the market-gardeners, which form a mosaic bowl of green round the outskirts of the city, with ragged indentations into that first Circle of Power, the industrial suburbs. This industrial circle is the outer structural support of a myriad-meshed web of lives inside it: like the rim of a wheel. Here the mechanical pressure on the green country is completed. The gardens become narrow backyards, smutted by the furnace-chimneys that drop heavy shadows over them. Like grass under a stone, their produce has no chlorophyll; pallid, swollen vegetables reared under glass like bacilli in a laboratory. Here are the catacombs of mushroom-growers. From here comes the livid asparagus of Argenteuil. The residue of the forests that have ventured to this region is squeezed out of orifices between the giant cells of these factories to make the Paris Avenues, and sent on in parallel rays across shrieking tram-lines, under groaning cranes, down dreary combes of drink and bicycle shops, through the abandoned pents of the old fortifications, centrewards. In this labyrinthine corridor Landru had his run and his home-earth.

From the points where they cut the circumference of Paris, the lanky lines of trees are ruled by straight-edge in a hundred radials to the hub, which is the Bourse and the banking quarter of ferroconcrete palaces. Here is the other structural element of the city, the roaring vibrating money quarter, from the steps of whose Greek temple goes out at all the noon hours a clamour louder than an orchestra of steam-hammers; the axle of Paris, the buyers and sellers of shares.

Round this Bourse focus at various tangents, drawn by history of numerous centuries, are all the great lineaments of the city. Southwards, in a shaky line, the ruins of a land-owning feudality, the Boulevard St. Germain, pious and old, doubled by the logical terrace of the Ministries, the Parliament, the Academy, beginning with the shrine of the Army, the Invalides, and ending with the Law Courts and Notre-Dame. Northwards is the freehand vector of the industry of amusement, which starts in a dazzle of electricity on the Boulevards, shades away quickly through the equivocal bars of Lorette, and the rendez-vous parlours of St. Lazare, blazes up again for a moment

on the heights of Montmartre, a bonfire for the whole
world, then, damped down every yard, along the straight
strategical boulevards round the Gare de l'Est, it fades at
last into the gloomy prostitution of the Outer Barrier,
where the great shadows of the factory walls begin again.
In every segment, chord, diameter of this living diagram
Landru had in his lifetime business; its entire population
followed his fate with passion and allied in his punishment. His hunt led him up the narrow back stairs that lie
behind the palaces, his longings and sins knew both the
staring lights of the theatre quarter, where he found Fernande Segret, and the clandestine perfumes of certain
rooms near by, where he met Andrée Babelay, the palmist's assistant. When he was young and a choir boy he
loved Notre-Dame. When he was a young man, his dossier
and his profile portrait were stacked handily in the file
drawers of the Paris Prefecture. His hopes were at the
Bourse-Centre, his garage at the Industrial-Rim, his trade
at remote Gambais; Academicians, Duchesses, Actresses
fought to stare at him on trial with the miscellaneous riff-
raff who live on holiday. The working people of Paris
envied them. They would much rather have witnessed
Landru march down the Champs Élysées than the Allied
Prime Ministers.

A whole city, a whole time thus seems after a ghastly
and mocking manner to be summed up in this individual,
or at any rate to have a distorted reflection in him. No flat
mirror passive in itself could have achieved this function;
no nonentity. Landru was certainly a personality; if not a
vehicle of power: a living allegory of large and obvious

content, in which millions of nerve-racked, disillusioned men recognized a hideous likeness, and being momentarily without dignity, were forced to laugh at it, as if they had discovered an ape successfully masquerading as one of themselves.

The personality of Landru, and the extraordinary social phenomenon of his reaction on his times are both to be studied together. Paris in 1919 was, more than all the other capitals of the world, a city of survivors. Every citizen counted his limbs and was amazed to be alive. Every one, when the cannons on the Seine fired their blanks for victory, started out of a hypnotic nightmare that had lasted four years, or like a Crusoe home at last threw himself with joy into that latest scandal of the village which assured him of his return. Returned soldiers, reading of Landru, heard for the first time since they entrained of the old things, the old games, the old scenes which they were hungry to re-explore. They read of concierges, of palmists, of whores and cooks and Saturday nights; all the traditional puppets of civilian life, the libretto of a pantomime they had half forgotten. They heard the old jokes, now attributed to Landru. They followed with delighted recollection the street names in the accounts of Landru's crimes. This host back from killing, or suddenly relieved from the fear of being killed, with the taste of despair still under their tongues, learnt with a roar that a little funny man had all these years behind their backs been conducting a private war of his own, earnestly mimicking theirs, even to the casualties. Four years of intermittent abstinence had made all the men women-hungry, all the women starved for men; the very mention of their old sport of Love raised their hysterical laughter to a shout. In the court, when the Prosecutor in his charge came to the statement 'Landru had relations with 284 women,' we heard that cry: admiration, regret, desire, which the fathomless law of human expression turns into prolonged hilarity. It lasted until the Judge, who had orders to extend his natural patience, prepared to clear the court. All these were reasons for the passionate interest of the Paris public in Landru. The case was the lay Te Deum for resurrection, the horseplay festival of peace, indecent as birth, stupid as war, unrulable and spontaneous as all the movements of the mob. On the whole it profited public order. It straightened the forehead of the surly combatant, ready to massacre the profiteers who had won where he had lost, this immense joke on all the *embusqués*. It was also a good joke against themselves. They howled loudest of all when they noticed Landru had a trench-beard like themselves; in a twinkling this badge of their past sufferings and deceptions was shaved off every face: with it the *Poilu* surrendered the badge of his dangerous segregation from the rest of the nation.

The established forces of government, the press of information and the oligarchy of Clemenceau and Mandel seized willingly on the opportunity. The newspapers, bewildered at the sudden absence of a war communiqué, flung themselves eagerly on this first peace-news. The ironic despot himself, charmed with the discovery of a screen to push in front of the plans for a peace settlement he wished to elaborate undisturbed, gave murky instructions to the police and the magistrates to 'cherish the Landru case.' The mob in cry after their murderer did not notice, or were delighted to notice, the concomitant shortness of news about the Peace Conference. The raging protests of the liberals of all the opposition at the fantastic doings of the tyrant, in high politics, so found no echoes. Clemenceau carried to an end the French participation in the Treaty of Versailles—with the help of Landru—who thus unexceptionally enters into political history at its modern turn-point.

The intersection of Landru's fate-line with public history lay in a china-shop, the 'Lions de Faience,' in the Rue de Rivoli: more precisely, on the left hand of the cash-throne, at the end of an alley of pots and glasses, from which, as he spoke to the cashier, he could be seen by a person standing at the other end, though barred off by a crowd of shopping women. It was the 12th of April 1919, a Saturday. This shop (to attenuate the accident) is not an insignificant place, but one of the very numerous institutions around which the doings of Paris tend to collect; not *any* china-shop, but the one place in the city where broken sets of out-of-issue pattern may be completed. At one of the restaurants in the Bois, a patient customer may confidently expect to meet sooner or later any particular moneyed pleasure seeker in the world. At the shop in the Rue de Rivoli, if you wait long enough, you may count on re-meeting any woman of the lesser French bourgeoisie, once at least in her lifetime, and most of their husbands, all who have ever received a wedding present of a dinner-service and employed a servant who can crack a cup.

On Saturdays the goods on display are retired half an inch from the edge of the shelves, to avoid breakages;

Mademoiselle Lacoste was unable to cleave the crowd in the direction of the man she had recognized. But from a hundred tea-sets away, she identified his fawn-coloured beard, his polished scalp when he lifted his hat, his attitude, which was as unmistakable as his step if she could have heard it above the loud confusion of a great shop in full sale. As soon as she might, she veered under the cashier and asked and received from her the name of the polite customer. He was one Guillet, Lucien, engineer, 76 Rue de Rochechouart on the hither slope of Montmartre, who had bought a tea-service for his wife, to be sent immediately to his flat. Mademoiselle heard the name with grim unbelief, then, like a lean middle-aged Angel of Vengeance, stepped out to the nearest Commissariat of Police to announce that, unaided by all their efforts of the past months, she herself had at least found the address of Fremyet, engineer; abductor, seducer, sequestrator and, in her suspicion, slayer of her sister Widow Buisson. Also in all probability of the so-called Dupont, suspected of the same offenses on the sister of Madame Collomb, with which lady she was in relations since the coincidence of the place, Gambais, from which both women had disappeared, had been revealed to her by the magistrate charged with investigation into her own case.

The Commissioner received the information with mediocre enthusiasm, but sent her on to the Central Bureau. Here they were more interested, mainly because of certain identities in the description of this Fremyet or Dupont or Guillet with a swindler named Landru for whom they had been long in search. The next morning two detectives went to the given address, above a jeweller's shop, a small neat flat, there arrested Guillet, who made no trouble about admitting his real name was Henri Desiré Landru (Nandru, the first Press reports have it), fugitive from a sentence of a criminal court for fraud in 1913. With him they took away his companion, a tall, ugly girl, very coquettish, named Fernande Segret, who wept all the short time of her detention. In the afternoon, the two were brought back in a cab to their flat, to be present at the impounding of their papers; when that long operation was finished the man asked to be allowed to take his leave of Fernande, whom he understood was immediately to be released. He kissed her and according to a strong legend, which she herself supports, said or hummed, with an operatic gesture and a 'pale smile,' the favourite little melody from 'Manon Lescaut': *'Adieu, notre petite table.'*

With this verse the Landru case began. Whether or not the incident, at that place and time, was true, whether, after he had seen the brigadier turn over, at first curiously, then carefully, the leaves of the twopenny notebook covered with black waxed cloth that lay on top of the drawer, Landru could so have mastered his despair as to remember to be true to character, and even emblematical, it is now a matter of temperament to decide. It is certain, and as historic as anyone could wish, that the story that this handcuffed man under suspicion of two murders took leave from his mistress with the best known sentimental phrase of the best known sentimental opera in Paris, was handed to the reporters by the police the next day, and because of its 'news-value' placed Landru for the first time on the front page of the Press. The great public—and the whole of the unwritten art of newspaper production holds in this—always reserves its interest for the things it already knows. The incident of a tune which every midinette had in her heart in an affair not obviously at this stage remarkable, explains the early precipitation of the Press on the Landru story. Next day when the 'lost-dog' reporters called again for news and heard that the accused Landru was something of a wit, a fish that showed fight and would need playing, they knew that the first real peace news had arrived, and sorrowed to realize that the special correspondents would take its further course out of their hands.

To a chosen pack of these latter, Monsieur Dautel, commissioner in charge of the case, now showed the notebook itself. This dirty little thing, which the detectives had found on their second visit to the flat in the Rue Rochechouart, was one of the prime properties of the case, almost equally with the phrase from Manon. The one is a clue to the depths of Landru's mind; the other contained, as you shall see, the whole police case against him. It was ruled in money-columns in the customary pale blue ink. It was almost covered with a close writing in pencil, most of it the petty accounts of a methodical man; but near the beginning was this strange inscription jotted across the lines:

A. Cuchet. G. Cuchet. Brésil. Crozatier. Havre. C.t. Buisson. A. Colomb. Andrée Babelay. M. Louis Jaume. A. Pascal. M. Thr. Marcadier.

Dautel pointed out the significant occurrence in this abracadabra of the names Pascal and Collomb, or Colomb, as it was spelt, two missing women, whose sisters had already formally recognized in Landru the lacking Dupont and Fremyet. Further, the name Buisson corresponded with that of another woman, reported by her family as missing in September, 1917. This woman's concierge had been put before Landru and had recognized him as a constant visitor to her vanished tenant.

The accounts were all on this pattern:

> Expenses of 25th Decembre.
> 2 Metro tickets, returns.
> Invalides, 0,40.
> One single 3,95.
> One return 4,95.
> One ticket (single Tacoi) 2,75.
> Ticket (return) 4,40.
> 13th March.
> 2 tickets (return) 9,90.
> 27th April.
> Meeting f. Pascal 4,90.
> Biscuits, Malaga.
> 4th April.
> Invalides, cab 3.
> Tickets 3,10—4,95.
> Post-chaise 2,40.
> Houdan (St. Lazare), 10 francs.
> 18th January.
> Post-chaise (Diligence) 1,75.

From these entries the police were able to trace successively ten persons who had disappeared after relations with Landru. It is convenient at this point to give their names and some description of them, together with others not mentioned in the notebook.

WIDOW CUCHET claimed to be thirty when she met

Landru in 1914. She was a domestic servant with a son of sixteen or seventeen, and several thousand francs of savings, of which Landru quickly defrauded her, but was pardoned months before her final disappearance. Widow Cuchet had no more colour or taste than water; from January 1915 to the day that the police seized the notebook it was as if she and her son had evaporated.

WIDOW GUILLIN, a respectable woman of fifty-one, with a fortune estimated by her family at 40,000 francs, lonely and discontented, disappeared two months later.

WIDOW BERTHE HEON, who came from Havre (and is apparently included in the list under that name), was fifty-four years old. She lived in a small shabby *milieu* of old women with incomes. She disappeared three months after Widow Guillin.

WIDOW COLLOMB was of higher social class. She was the 'woman in a blue silk dressing-gown' in the case, that is, it was she who was seen by neighbours of the Gambais villa in the walled garden in that attire for a few mornings before she too vanished. In her life was one of those incidents which are only romantic because of the exotic names in them: she had had a child by a lover in Guatemala, who was being educated in a convent at San Remo.

ANDRÉE BABELAY, a servant girl nineteen years old, who worked for a palmist in the St. Lazare quarter. A big lumping hussy, whose case stands by itself, for she had no money.

WIDOW JAUME, from the quarter of small tradesmen and skilled workmen, Belleville. A stout, sentimental woman of forty-two, whom Landru wooed with flowers.

Then ANNETTE PASCAL, an Arlésienne, with large black eyes and false teeth. Landru's denunciatrice, Mademoiselle Lacoste, was her sister.

MARIE THÉRÈSE MARCHADIER, known in the brothels of various garrison towns as La Belle Mythèse, still flamboyant at thirty-seven. She had wisely saved enough out of her military admirers to equip a small hotel in the interminable Rue St. Jacques; it was in a negotiation for the sale of this business that she met Landru.

There were others: MADAME LABORDE-LINE, who came from Buenos Aires (hence Brésil in the list!); WIDOW BENOIST, or BENOIT, a buxom cashier at a 'beuglant'—one of the lesser music-halls near the Rue de la Gaiété. Others again whose names filled for a day a column of sensation, then dropped out of the case, either because they had been traced or from inability of the police to find anything definite about them. Effaced, half-existent women, all of them, whose personality was not strong enough to leave even a distinct trace in the memories of their friends.

These identifications by the police were not at all simultaneous. Intervals of weeks, sometimes months, separated them. Each as it was announced had the air of a present to the public, a treat in reward for its patience over the interminable negotiations of the Peace Conference, which on such occasions became a secondary affair. Paris was thus fed irregularly with rich and indigestible repasts of blood and sex: perhaps the only food which its enervated palate could have stood. Often the announcement of the finding of a new 'fiancée,' the spiced details of her seduction by the strange creature in the cage at the

Santé, exciting guesses at the way of her murder, would unaccidentally coincide with the bare announcement of the latest decision of the Big Four; so with red jam the nasty pilule would pass down. There was a conjuration of chance in favour of the cranky despots who were making the treaty; the debasement of the currency, the badgering of Germany into life, the licence to all the hobbyists of Europe to create and kill nationalities at their fancy, the mass-betrayals and bribings, the huge spree with the profits of the deaths of 12,000,000 men, which left not only Europe but Asia in more certain danger of war than it was in 1914: these were all safely smuggled, as far as the population in whose midst they were done were concerned, under the mackintosh-tails of our seedy little murderer. With them the minor villainies of the Clemenceau Government, the methodical perpetration of all the private revenges of the worst hater in France. A reign of terror carried out by Ignace and Mandel, hung over the politicians of the country; scores dating from the days of Cornelius Herz and Panama were being repaid, and the Santé was full of other prisoners. But the great public were interested in no one but Landru.

In the moment of destiny, the French had their heads buried in a feuilleton.

At least, its central figure, this Landru, could rival in his life and character most of the personages in past *romans à succès*. With a little jogging from the journalists, the examining magistrate had fixed the main traits of his subject: Landru's deep and luminous eyes, his hypnotic charm, his inflexible assurance, his wit, his mystery; and Landru did his best to live up to this schedule. Even when he stood in full light before the reporters at Versailles, they continued to write about his 'black beard,' though it was too obviously a tawny ginger, because the public expected a black beard in its satyr. His *'rouspetance'* was doctored by able wits, and when it failed into a grumpy silence or mere insolences, epigrams were attributed to him, some say from canonical anecdotes of Clemenceau himself. The mawkish was out of fashion; in those days Landru gave us what we wanted. As Clemenceau did, he faced his horrors as we wished we could, with a bright eye, a rasping tongue, a sang-froid which had a savour of desperate rebellion. 'Prove it,' he would answer contemptuously to the magistrate when a new abomination in his past was spread traitorously in front of him. 'I'm a man of honour, and won't say,' was all threats and wheedling could ever find out about the ends of these sinister idylls. When they shook his notebook, his damnation, in his face (the reports told us) they could get nothing from him but a laugh, a real laugh, and a waggish 'I must have been a thrifty man.'

By skins as an onion is peeled, the detectives opened up each of his impostures, towards the first facts of his boyhood and birth. Born in Paris, in the 19th arrondissement, in 1869—year of Troppmann's death. His father was a stoker at the *Forges de Vulcain,* a self-bettering man; all identifiable trace of his mother has disappeared. Desiré Landru was 'un petit garçon très doux, très timide et très caressant.' In his embryo is indeed little of the finished grotesque that the whole of 1919 is jabbering about. Perhaps only this, that he was too shy to play with other boys. He had a sweet voice, and the clergy, who esteem this type of boy, soon found him and gave him a place in the choir of St. Louis-en-l'Île, where he sang alto to Sunday nave-fulls of Bonapartist tradesmen. His voice cracked late, when he was fifteen years old. The curé, to keep him, allowed him to serve the mass, and wear a dalmatic at the festivals, whence the tradition that he was actually received to the order of sub-deacons. When he was sixteen, he passed the entrance examination of the École des Arts-et-Métiers which prepares for the profession of mechanical engineering: here again there is a vague echo of his later life, for his favourite imposture was to take the part of an engineer; and he was always ready with impressive technical words. He was conscripted before he had qualified. He was sent to the garrison town of St. Quentin, where his punctuality and submission, qualities prized by officers as well as priests, soon gained him sergeant's stripes. With the idea of shortening his time with the colours, after four years he married, and soon after was released to civilian life. Meanwhile his father had yielded to lifelong ambition and joined the collared classes. He had abandoned the factory, and found precarious work as a publisher's canvasser; and Desiré, on his return was obliged to follow him upwards. Besides, there was now no more money to support him for the final year at the school; young Landru was placed as book-keeper and general clerk. So for years the family added chapters that matched each other.

But in 1900, the year of the Exhibition, the father being feverishly occupied with the thousand new chances it had the air of bringing to his career, Desiré Landru went into a metamorphosis which changed him from the sentimental, softish fellow hitherto into an impudent swindler. This change, instead of having no explanation, as many have said, has too many. They range from the magical hypothesis of the alienists: that Landru must have fallen off a ladder, or in another way received a blow on the head, which blow or accident there was a great bother to find.

The undoubted antecedence of the theory to the evidence makes the latter, and its explanatory worth, very suspect. In the history not only of remarkable persons such cracks are common. Before accepting them as sufficient causes for the strange and sudden changes that make mass-murderers out of mild book-keepers, or (as it has been done) saints out of wastrels, and poets out of pig-keepers, other less alarming possibilities must be explored. Much of modern criminological theory, like the earlier nonsense of Lombroso that they have, under pressure of ridicule, discarded, certainly comes from the baseless and unconscious pride of honest men who refuse to see in a felon a like animal to themselves, of like instincts, feelings, methods, a lost straggler from the army, not an alien tribesman. If anyone wishes to cure himself of this error, let him, in the privacy of the night, set himself the little exercise of reckoning, in his own life, the exact number of years' imprisonment he himself would have accomplished had he unfortunately been caught in every lawless act, even the most insignificant, and had had the misfortune of being sentenced on such occasions to the maximum penalty of the law. It is not necessary to add to this the probably unsound evangelic reckoning of all crimes of intention, though the total from this latter method will assist powerfully in seeing the resemblance. 'There, quite conceivably, go I,' the majority of honest men, with awe if not piety, may say to most petty swindlers and thieves as they stumble down from dock to prison. And from swindlers to the lowest hell which we are visiting there is, as we have found, a quite practicable path down. So, in this case of Desiré Landru we will not believe that he is a hand-watch that one bang on the case deranged, but that he came under a law of metabolism that works, though in infinitely varying degrees and periods, in the lives of all human beings. At the age of thirty years, quite an ordinary period for a man to reflect on his life, measure his situation, and if he finds it displeasing reform it, this Landru reviewed, we may legitimately suppose, his past and present, and then firmly decided to try another road to the future.

The slow accumulation of his experience had come to persuade him that submission did not pay. The sight of the unusual luxury and heightened life that the Exhibition brought to the city sharpened his desires, and by natural maturity, his adoration of ecclesiastical scents and sounds and sights had developed into other desires which promised less vague and more realizable satisfactions. He knew he needed more money, more freedom, more solitude from men and more of the company and pleasures of women. So he set himself to his first small fraud, which prospering, another, and so on until, with a terrible shock, no doubt, he found himself at his first conviction, in 1900, in Paris. It is still confidently hoped that two years' hard labour is the right medicine for a case like this; once more it failed.

It failed, not only because a prison condemnation makes the future exercise of any honest trade or occupation difficult, except that of the common labourer, but still more because of the mental obstacle of the convicted man's intimate way of thinking. If Landru considered that he was guilty, the terrible suffering of two prison years might frighten him from his ways, in spite of the after-difficulties of an honest life; but it is wrong to suppose that a swindler, a man who is rather more than less egotist than the normal, denies himself in the solitude of his cell from the almost universal pleasure of believing oneself in the right. The pupil Landru, like the fully-developed mass-murderer that he grew into later, not only found excuses for himself, in the personal causes of the action that had brought him there, and in the practical morality of the times around him, but he definitely considered that he had been unjustly injured for a piece of sharp business in no way out of the ordinary. So the mill of the law has failed with him. It turned him out still harder than he went into its maw. He is caught again in 1904 for the same offense, and given another two years' hard labour; then in 1906, thirteen months; then in 1909, three years; then at Lille, in the same year while serving the sentence, another three years; finally, on the 20th July 1914, he was sentenced, by default, for fraud to four years' imprisonment and *'rélega-tion,'* that is, lifelong obligation to reside in New Caledonia. It was to inflict on him the performance of this sentence that the police were looking for him throughout the war period. The manner of his frauds showed a nice gradation in the art of the confidence trick, with a noticeable tendency to choose victims among women, and these of a certain age and sort. It may be laid down that in Landru's pre-war career the women always grew older and uglier, and that his means of meeting them narrowed more and more to the columns of the newspaper. In his last bloodless case, the fixed type is reached: he advertised for second-hand furniture, met an elderly widow and bilked her of payment for the sale of her goods.

Here, openly, is a resemblance between Landru and English Smith: both second-hand dealers, both preying on women. They were, in fact, in the same branch of trade, which will make their dissimilarities the more interesting. His last condemnation had made Landru a desperate, hunted man; only the war, and the general disorganization of the police service that followed its outbreak, saved him from a living death in Cayenne. For he was like all his class, an animal that had his habits; the hunters were perfectly aware of his appearance as well as his methods and forms, even of the stereotyped formulæ of his advertisement. August 1914, though it saved his skin, almost ended him by hunger. All business in these first months ceased. There was no one to sell or buy, and Landru, slinking about the outer labyrinth of Paris, was hard put to it to get a meal a day. Even a day may hold many resolutions to a destitute man; it was on 14th August 1914 that he appears to be in the midst of his first murder. With most of our other specimens there was a pause, a hesitation before the jump from their thieving to their killing, well marked and full of terrific meaning. The famished Landru hardly checks his step. Sooner or later, on the way he was going, he was bound to stump his nose against the barrier that separates crime into two parts, when in the course of a deception he was certain to notice and ponder that the logical conclusion of a fraud was to kill the victim, and so take, not a pittance, but the whole. In the days of mobilization, with starvation at his heels, Landru does not even check at it, but bursts through as if it were made of smoke. In a few days he met the Widow Cuchet and her son André, deceived them, trapped them, robbed them, and abolished them. On 14th August he is selling a tobacco-pipe belonging to the boy; in January 1915 mother and son are vanished from the earth, from the stepping-stone of a villa which Landru hired in Vernouillet, a village in the *villégiature* zone of the city. By July of the same year, the last possessions of the unfortunate couple were sold, and in the following month he is in the midst of the murder of the Widow Guillin. Somewhere hidden, not only by the obscurity of deeds done without witnesses, but (far more) by the speed, he had juggled his way across that gap which held up Smith and Troppmann, so long.

In two other characteristics Landru leaves that impression of hocus-pocus which was behind the name one of his victim's friends gave him of 'Mr. Mystery.' There was the conjuring away of his bodies, which I will discuss; and then there was his fascination of women. First we must clear away the charlatanry, his own and that which hurried journalists wrapped round him. Landru's magnetic eyes were a fable; they were only queer eyes, two shining black spots at the bottom of depressions, fixed unchanging objects that appeared artificial as if he had been fitted with two glass eyes, of a fanciful make, rather than the eyes of a dominator or seducer. These eyes gave no confidence, but rather the effect of an infirmity. Unless women are to be fascinated by curiosity alone, they had no part in his success. Landru's whole look, in fact, does not explain even the humblest of his conquests. He was a shabby, bowed little man, fitted for peddling or any form of selling in which pity besides business has to matter. As to his manner, that is different. His speech was highly persuasive to a certain class of women and young persons, for he had a great deal of calm, always based himself on the most assimilable form of reason, Law, and ornamented every statement with technical words which gave them an appearance of great dignity. When in argument, he would not allow the contradictor to state his own case, but he would do it for him quickly and fairly, then demolish it, gravely and sometimes with an expression of sympathetic regret. In his walk and when standing, he contrived by slowness and deliberation to expunge the last trace of anything ridiculous in his seediness, by which it appeared to many merely another mark of distinction, as if he was a millionaire too preoccupied to trouble about clothes. His poor physique often prepossessed women among whom a certain thinness is instinctively believed to be a sign of a sort of worldly innocence that disarms mistrust and calls for protection. Many of Landru's women felt he needed protection. On the whole, then, Landru gave the impression in his world of a distinguished gentleman, poor, perhaps, but learned and serious, as it were an unofficial professor, whose crankiness was very respectable. Even in the court of Versailles many of the witnesses, and—supreme tribute—among them concierges, could not bring themselves to speak of the poor devil standing between gendarmes in the dock on their right otherwise than as *'Monsieur'* and *'Ce monsieur.'* This effect indeed was not universal: certain families, among them the Lacostes and the Collombs, people of a higher social rank than the rest, to whose coalition besides Landru owed his arrest, disliked him from the start, and may even, as they declared in court, have taken him to be 'a very fishy person' when they met him in the company of their enthralled sisters. But it was true for the majority of those humbler women with whom he had contact; it would partly explain how those 'sou-gripping' charwomen could have so tamely lost their heads to his frauds. But there was much more in Landru, much that cannot be explained, either by his quackery, or still less by any erotic superstition about him. This second charm can be put: that he knew what he was after in life. To women (I am not sure of men) this is doubtless the strongest lure in the world. However it is looked at: that Landru had will, or direction, or a theory, or a belief, it means in practice that he was positive to the same degree that they were negative, and so they followed him, as by an electromagnetic law, or as one man walking firmly and straight through a crowd of saunterers will draw them infallibly after him. All the women whom he destroyed were completely lacking in this purpose: the young Babelay unconsciously, her elders with the sting of knowing that they had few more years in which to discover the secret without which they were mere flotsam. This man who had overawed them with his supposed culture drew them pantingly after him with the hope that he possessed the plan they had missed; he promised to let them share it with him in marriage. Again it must be observed that the bait was not simply, or even chiefly, one of the senses; most of them were widows, none virgins, and even at fifty a woman who desires sexual intercourse in Paris need not go to the point of making an advertisement for marriage to enjoy it without publicity. The marriage offer that Landru set out was perfectly understood by both parties to include much wider benefits than "love": to the woman it meant the whole of that vast range of benefits that the institution everywhere endows her; lifelong financial support, as the least though solidest, and still more (for they were all self-supporting) whatever deep needs of human kind are expressed by 'company'—which in the case of this man meant a full share in the secret and meaning of life which everything, from his absent eyes to his confident walk, advertised that he possessed. They fell on Landru, as lost trippers in an artificial labyrinth will cling to a passer who says and shows that he knows the way to the centre. Past the menopause, all of them, they knew— counting back from the unreality to which they had come, a life entirely meaningless and useless, in which they were not even happy—that every single act since they were born, their sleep, their work, their sufferings, was equally unreal. They had not even that last means of illusion in the life of a woman, that last substitute for a purpose, a man to themselves. In ordinary times, this bitter consciousness would have been unobtrusive, lulled by the comfortable materialism around them of millions who left the Sphinx's riddle alone. But a war to a spinster is like a ball in the house next door, a wild and fascinating carousal of sound and adventure to which she has not been invited. Let no one, pacifist or patriot, imagine that the masses read the war communiqués. But in huge Paris there was talk of death, and purpose which is life, and in a conglomerated object of their despairing envy, these women heard of death and purpose, which is life, of enfolding words, sacrifice, duty, democracy. There were drums in the air, which made it a frenzy to be alone. Age, sex and time were in complicity with Landru. He was the male, the master of the secret.

They knew he had it, because of his air, because of his eyes (that did not move like their own), because he told them so, and because he believed it himself. To this pedler these peaked seekers were clients come to offer a bad bargain. Their wrinkled cheeks and dyed hair, their sticks of furniture and savings, together with the make-weight of their intimacy, against the fabulous value of his possession, himself and his secret. He had no more doubts than sun and moon, otherwise the spell had never been.

But what it was he believed, the nature of the charm in his possession that would have made the life of a washerwoman and a superannuated whore at last worth living, is more obscure. That these uneducated women never could discover it, and had to content themselves until the brutal end with mere hints, need not discourage all investigation; nor that the drama-drunk audiences at Versailles, and the hasty mob of reporters, and even the judges and pleaders intent on their own ambitions never guessed it, and felt that Mr. Mystery was well named. For these were all burning the Guy of Paris in the bonfire of their return, in clothes which they had themselves dressed him. An effigy of their old bogy, the Satyr of the Bois de Boulogne: their mood was not for research, but a hilarious hunting. He was the resuscitation of the national joke against sexual impotence, this man who had 'had relations with two hundred and eighty-four women,' which lies as deep in the French subconsciousness as its brother, the fear of being a cuckold, in England. Covered with traditional rags, daubed with the traditional paints, the mysterious little fellow on his carnival throne was as safe from observation as he had been at Gambais. Even now the revellers have gone, it is a daring thing to pick about among his embers for his great secret, for it was deeply embedded in that ultimate cubby-hole of any human man, his personality. If it were not that he had himself half betrayed it to one woman, and that woman, Fernande Segret, worked by a mixed motive of her poverty and her notoriety, had not given it to us in a curious little pamphlet of her *Memoirs,* we might turn in despair from the search. We have this document. In it like an insect in a thick glass bottle we can vaguely see this queerest of mass-murderers moving to and fro and study him at ease.

At first, in these *Memoirs,* it is only the minor interest of his ways and wiles that catches our attention: his manner of approach, the system of his lies, how he behaved when seized by an angry and respectable mother, or how he looked after a return from a Saturday to Monday, which we know from an easy comparison of dates must have been filled with one of his black idylls at Gambais. Such passages as this satisfy our lesser curiosities:

Arrived at our destination, scarcely had we gone a
few yards on the pavement when a man accosted us,
saluted us very respectfully, and addressing himself to
me, with a voice whose charm and softness surprised me,
asked if we would allow him to accompany us for a few
minutes. It was the unknown of the tramcar [who had
stared at Fernande Segret and her friend fixedly a short
time before]. We refused the invitation with a smile, and
quickened our pace to get away from him. But our follower would not be shaken off. Rather cheekily he sug-
gested that young girls in Paris go out all too often alone,
with the risk of being accosted by bad characters and all
sorts of annoyances from men. Such a statement made us
laugh loudly; our follower took advantage of it to stay.
As we were certain we would soon give him the slip, we
exchanged some commonplaces with him. He talked on,
abundantly, with a most lively wit, and every subject he
touched on he seemed to be at home in.

On a later occasion, Fernande again meets the man,
Landru, who 'confided to me that he was a manufacturer,
owner of an automobile and of a garage near Paris, and
of a sweet little villa at Gambais where he liked to do a
rest cure from time to time. My father, he said, was a
very rigid and austere man, and always kept my mother
ignorant of his business. I suffered much, for I had a
boundless affection for her. . . . His eyes shone as he
spoke of his mother, and he gave the impression of
much emotion.'

Fernande Segret, who '*subissait les apprehensions
d'une époque où la guerre laissait aux jeunes filles peu
d'espoir sur leur avenir,*' allowed him to call on her family,
whom he charmed with gifts of flowers and genteel, grave
ways. He claimed to be a refugee from the war region, by

which he explained the lack of identity papers, necessary before there could be a marriage. Here is a party at the Segrets', which is as curious in its way as the grasshopper's method of laying its eggs.

> The following Wednesday we were all seated with him at a family dinner. Grandfather was with us, and I noticed at once by his happy smile how much he appreciated the lively conversation of Lucien [Lucien Guillet, Landru's pseudonym in the incident] and how much he liked the many attentions which his neighbour at the table showered on him. That evening Lucien was dazzling in his "go" and comicalities. Without ever forgetting that he was in the presence of ladies, he poured out jokes, witty retorts, and even juggled for us with the napkin rings in a clever way, all the time garnishing his talk with the most wonderful puns. At dessert, as we were on the subject of music halls, he recalled the triumphs of stars of the past, whom he had known, and sang for us some lines of a once famous song *"Le Bal à l'Hôtel de Ville."* So he attracted the liking of all and no one had eyes all the evening for anyone but Monsieur Lucien.

This impression, so obviously authentic in its reporting, Landru added to by many another device. 'We were at the critical moment of food restrictions. Neither *petits fours* nor pastry were any way to be had, but nevertheless he managed always to bring us all these prohibited delicacies, and when we showed our delighted surprise, he would answer that if one really wanted anything, one could always get it.'

At the house-warming of his flat in the Rue Rochechouart:

There an unforgettable spectacle shone on our eyes. It was not a mere flat on which the door opened, it was a real greenhouse. The dining room was nothing but an immense basket of flowers. I have never seen such a display, in size or variety. He had with careful taste mixed humble violets with the rarest gardenias, and everything was so well arranged, with such harmonies of colours, such taste in the bouquets, that mother and I looked at it as if we were paralysed. "You must have robbed the Nice flower train," I said at last. . . .

Finally the difficulties of the identity papers having been recognized as insuperable, Fernande avows that she went to live with him, in the flat at the Rue Rochechouart, with the tacit permission of her mother. After some time, 'Lucien' asked her to visit his little property in Gambais. They went down by train, and hired bicycles at the station of Gambais.

At last we passed the cemetery, and then, before we entered the village, Landru waved to a little house, buried in the trees, still far off and murmured to me, happily: "There is my little paradise."
We jumped off our bicycles and entered the grounds. The garden seemed to me very large, but it was completely neglected. A few half-wild roses, some geraniums run to seed in a jungle of weeds and bushes.

At this point Fernande, after having inspected the house, which was practically without furniture, and where 'none of the rooms seemed to be used for what it was intended,' makes the characteristic remark: 'Wouldn't it be possible to let my family come and live here?' It was the high season for the Gotha raids. But Landru evasively refused.

These and fifty other such passages show the value of this little document, saved from banality by the happy simplicity both of the narrator and the editor. It allows us to see the greatest murderer of our times with limpidity, as he went about his business. For though it is certain that this girl was in no immediate danger during this period, yet it is equally sure, both a priori and from fragmentary revelations in the evidence at the trial, that the manner, the technique employed by him in the snaring of his victims was the same. But this is only the husk of Landru, and having followed with delight the curious detail of his ways we must return to our deeper research of what he meant to the long muster of these unhappy women, and why.

For granted that Landru was in love with this girl who has given us his secrets, with her airs and simpers, as he assuredly never was with the elderly row of victims, with whose spoils she was thus elegantly seduced, on the other hand, she certainly was not in love with him, and the attentions over which she rolls such a greedy little tongue replaced with her accordingly the overwhelming, obscure passion which was the cord that held the others to Landru, whose roots we have set ourselves audaciously to explore. Again we have to thank the news-editor for light; without prompting from a skilled publicist trained in the tradition of *documents*, Fernande, the scatter-brain, would doubtless never have thought of giving us Landru's letters, which have the clue; nor perhaps of recalling that queer simulation of suicide which rushed to our help when we were almost turned back in despair. Here, first, is the letter which is reproduced in facsimile in the *Memoirs:*

Thursday evening.

I am, my pretty little friend, in a sorry state which
draws me near your caressing heart to find consolation
and forgetfulness of my pain. I must tell you that first of
all, mustn't I? Don't be alarmed, it's nothing you have
done, you would never do me harm; I myself am the
cause, but I cannot yet quite explain it. Yesterday I saw
your beautiful eyes, so deep, so stirring; clouded with a
little worry. I cannot ignore that I must have been the
cause since there was no one near except ourselves. But
what can it be? Can I have said a word, or a phrase that
shocked you? Or anything else of the many things that
I have been trying to think of, in vain? That is how I look
at it, and it leads me to examine many matters which in
my happiness at having you by my side I did not think
of, in the sheer joy of my heart at being filled with you.
Unfortunately implacable reason when one dissects it
shows a thousand things, perhaps mistaken, but perhaps,
ah me, nearer truth. From this number, I have excluded
the idea that you were hurt because I cannot bring you
a quite new love. Certainly your beautiful soul deserves
it, and I long to be able to do so. But we have promised
to be frank with each other and I will tell you everything
about myself which you would like to know, or which
it is good for you to know. But please, please don't press
me too soon. I am by nature, by life, by reason of my real
loneliness, spiritual and material, a hermit, and utterly
reserved. Perhaps you will find many new things in me,
more than you could suppose. It is for you who have so
much good sense to see that you don't ask too much
from me at a time, and I will see to it, in compensation
for all that hard experience has taught me, that no troubles you have and are good enough to confide in me can
touch you. Another of those hard truths which I have to
recognize, and which, perhaps, is one of the reasons, or
a part of one of the reasons, for your sadness, is the fact
that I am no longer of the same charming and hopeful
age as yourself. The years have been hard to me in all
the painful acceptation of the term; if I have kept a body

which is still supple and healthy I owe it only to a strict hygiene and to the avoidance of all excesses. Certainly I am still vigorous, more so perhaps than many a young man of our city, but the years have marked their imprint on me and I would take it as a stupidity to try to hide it. But for you, little friend, whose very walk is pretty, whose fresh smile and eyes have a right to happiness, to dream, can I have the right to consider myself even as a chance pal without presumption? Don't protest out of politeness. I know myself pretty well. If I have some qualities, I have also great faults, the balance is against me if I weigh them up. Only, if that could explain it all, a very great friendship, and, I fear, a feeling much deeper than affection draws me to you and grows daily as I find in you those precious treasures of the heart and head which I fear are so little appreciated in these times. Where am I going, little friend most dear, under your darling leading? and where are you pulling me? What will I be to you? What do you want to be to me? All these thoughts, all these reflections and a thousand others, as I have said above, make me try to find the reason for your little sadness. Tell me, beloved friend, and let your heart open a little. You will find, perhaps, a cure, certainly a friend who is indulgent, affectionate and attentive, whom you need never fear to come to whatever it may be. We don't know each other very well yet, but I have a presentiment that we will both learn to appreciate each other better in frank confidence. Would you like that? and isn't it too much to ask you? There are still other reasons that I have thought about, but those are more delicate and need to be discussed by word of mouth. They will not be mentioned by me unless I cannot find the reason for that cloud over your eyes, and when circumstances give me my chance.

Excuse my rambling prose, but the very thought of seeing you sad torments me. You alone can with one word calm me and give me back the so great happiness of seeing those deeply dreamy eyes, whose memory haunts me day and night, clear and sparkling once more.

Good-bye, don't make me wait too long; whatever your answer it will be welcome as coming from you and I will take it without a murmur. You will have, all the same, the respect, the good will, and if you wish—on your darling little hands, the best kisses of your

LUCIEN GUILLET.

Then, here is the mock suicide:

When he had gone, I shut the door quickly, almost sure that he would come back five minutes afterwards. I gave my visitor his leave, but hour after hour passed and there was no Lucien. On reflection, I imagined him so upset that suddenly I felt extremely miserable. I knew how bizarre he was, how complicated, and that day he had seemed so troubled that I asked myself whether perhaps he would not do something rash in his despair. That idea would not leave me; at last I began to think that he must have committed suicide. To reassure myself I decided to put on my hat and pay him a visit. It was about six o'clock in the evening. I found his door open, and timidly feeling my way in the darkened flat I entered. I called. No answer. Terrified, I hurried through the rooms one by one. Then, on his desk, placed so that they could not fail to catch the eye, I saw several leaves of paper with his writing on them—pieces of poetry, all expressing sadness and despair. Here is one of them which I remember:

Dieu, soutiens mon courage et chasse
    comme une ombre
Des biens que j'ai perdu le souvenir si doux.

On another page I then read these lines from the libretto of Gounod's "Faust":

Vains, echos de la joie humaine
Passez . . . passez votre chemin . . .

Slowly and hesitating, I then entered his room. On the sill I stopped. A really macabre scene had been prepared. In its usual place I found my photograph, bordered with crêpe, and in front of it a chair placed like a *prie-Dieu,* as if he must have been meditating there as one does before an idol or a holy picture. The floor was strewn with faded rose-petals. I was sorry now that I had not understood him. I bitterly regretted the harsh words I might have said to him, and I felt capable of anything to recall them, if there was still time. . . .

At this propitious point Lucien, who had been hiding in a cupboard, reappeared . . . and the chief chapter in their idyll commenced. Without the letter, I would still believe in the rose-petals on the floor, for it is only the finest of a thousand other incidents which, though decimated by criticism, can still rally enough survivors to prove that *this* was the Landru that sold shrewd housewives' possessions under their nose, and whom retired prostitutes—wariest of women-kind—followed to their death like hypnotized lambs. The elementary stages of his attraction can be arranged thus: (1) Landru—any man, who brought 'company' to solitary women marooned in exciting times, the petty swindler whose exemption from the trenches gave him, like thousands of others, an exceptional chance with the sex. (2) Landru—lodestone, the man with a purpose, in which these disoriented women longed to share. Here is his magnetism. But it is the honest magnetism of the compass, which has no truck with the supernatural.

Up to this point he shares with Smith, who we know used both these baits. Smith, too, presented himself to lonely women, and magnetized them with the positive goal they felt he possessed. It was not one in which they could possibly share—can indeed any mortal ever share the path another has found, or partake of his reality? The utter belief of both men in themselves, and confidence in their aim sucked in, dragged towards themselves and swirled in a rush the unsettled, groping wills of their victims. In Smith, as in Troppmann, as embryonically in Burke, no doubt, his goal was simple: to make a secure fortune for the self which he adored and pitied. But Landru has a more complicated heaven to which he no less remorselessly steers, and in return his net is of steel to their hempen ropes. Smith's women clung to him always when he was there, they wavered, as the story of Bessie Mundy showed, when he was away. The Kincks came to Troppmann's rendezvous, though they doubted and feared. But the satellites of Landru were as inexorably fixed to his personality as the outer and inner stars to their orbit and their sun. He was almost the founder of a religion; he was the equal in mastery with Rasputin, and Brigham Young, and the Old Man of the Mountains, the first assassin. This power of Landru, which went as far as death, was above that of his rivals in proportion to the height of his obsession over theirs, and its vastly wider content. This is the third spell of Landru, by which he traffics in immortal things, in the mysteries of life itself, and reveals himself to his bedazzled initiates as Landru—the Poet. I am ashamed to ask you to notice the abominable commonplaces of his letter and his *mise-en-scène,* and only because in translation some of them may have disguised themselves. His 'eyes clouded with a passing pain,' his

'charming and hopeful age,' his 'precious treasures of heart
and head,' his 'lonely soul,' and especially his years that
are 'hard in all the painful acceptation of the word,' need
no labels. His phrases are of the same atrocious banality
as the mechanism of his suicide, from the enshrined photograph of that poor slut, to the used lines from the
hackneyed opera. They are, on the other hand, much better than any of the letters, with which from time to time
our Press regales us, from Anglo-Indian subalterns to their
illicit loves in the Divorce Court; not only are they, I
suspect, much above the common level of middle-class
love letters, but in the *milieu* in which Landru lived, to
which he belonged, most commonplaces are rejuvenated
by their novelty and may be used and felt as expressions of
real feeling. Doubt not that they were so used, or that
Landru himself could smile at the old-fashioned details of
his love-game that conquered the sentimental Fernande.
To the poor widows of his intimacy, to himself, this man
was a poet, an artist. In his intercourse they felt the divine
glows of idealized emotion, which only Shakespeare and
Beethoven can give to the sophisticated: Landru's contact
brought perfumes unknown to them before from the very
bouquet of life. His presence had vague harmonies for
them of things they had heard faintly in their youth; his
talk was full of sweet words: loneliness, love, regret.
This he could do, because his own mind was full of them.
No one who has pored over the whole body of evidence in
the Landru trial and case can doubt that we are here
again in the presence of a self-deceiver, a being who has
fabricated out of his nature and his reading a dream, or

fiction of things, in which he is the hero, and in which he has fortified himself against reality by an ingenious rampart of lies. The only other view possible, that he was a perfectly awake murderer, that all his romanticism was hypocrisy, that is conscious falsification, easy as it would make the infliction of his punishment, only leaves his nature a mystery unparalleled in the animal world, wherein reasonable beings may not rest unless all explanations have been proved vain. Or it slides into a statement that he was mad, of which even his acute defender Maître Moro-Giafferi could find no evidence. The inner life of Landru was a day-dream, different only in furniture from that which Troppmann and Smith possessed, in that it was more poetic, more literary, than theirs. That it was inferior, trite poetry, and feuille-tonesque literature, does not allow of question. But even in their degradation, the arts do not entirely lose their character: there is a music of the roundabout, and the street song, and the proletariat of great sad modern cities have their folk-culture as well as the ancestral peasants, which though as degraded and adulterated as their food-stuffs, yet contrives in a way that should excite our wonder and pity to flavour and express that strange life. Landru brought to his women the sadness of a street-organ, the romance of a sentimental ballad, an assimilable mystery of the arts. For that ultimate reason they followed him as the animals followed the godlike piper of Thrace who afterwards too went down to hell. They were not drawn so far by anything altogether base. And this must have been his ulti-

mate secret. Nor to Landru was it base; he never meant
that they should share in it. He was deluded by his own
illusion. A sentimental love, going to music from Manon
Lescaut, perhaps this very late one for the gawky Fernande was his own goal, his sincere religion.

Which like a mystical tradesman he worked for by
day to enjoy by night. He had the protective faculty of
strictly separating business which had to be done from the
life for whose accomplishment he carried it on. As with
Smith, his stingy neatness is not a sign of an insensitive
man, but rather of the opposite: a man who cannot kill
or steal without hypnotizing himself with all the apparatus
of business. It is for this that we so often find, to his ruin,
a diary and petty accounts in the desk of a multi-mur-
derer. It was so with William Palmer, it was so with
Landru. And all of them were sustained in the anguish of
the dock by believing themselves back into pettifogging
business men and county court lawyers.

For at last the trial arrived, and we may turn our attention to Landru's great antagonist—Society. The daily
badgering of the monster in his cage by the examining
magistrate had lasted from 13th April 1919 to November
1921. His use to the Government had ended, for the dictatorship had fallen long ago, the people were restive for
their final treat. But all this racking had not drawn out
of the man a secret, the only one the examiners hoped
for, how he had disposed of his corpses. The villa at
Gambais had been excavated and sacked from rafters to
cellar, without any result but a handful of charred bones
which only cranks in the anatomy school could swear were

not rabbits' bones. The kitchen stove, on which the spiritual eyes of 30,000,000 people were fixed ever since Sal-
mon the reporter had playfully hinted that Landru might
have used it as a private incinerator, had been dismounted
and brought as a trophy; on Landru's own suggestion, the
discomfited experts had scraped the soot out of the chim-
ney for analysis, with no better result. Landru, like Smith,
would have to be condemned only on coincidence.

   This failure of the investigators undoubtedly worried
the responsible minister, that is a certain Monsieur Ignace,
the chief tool of the dictatorship. Landru had been extremely useful, but it would never do to allow him to be
acquitted, ridiculously, as was likely to happen in Paris,
where criminal juries are always dramatic. As a terribly
sure safeguard from this possibility, Ignace sent the trial
to Versailles. The Versailles juries seldom err in mercy;
they are drawn from a population of small farmers, ren-
tiers, and master-workmen who believe in the law. From
the moment of that decision Landru was as doomed as if
infected with a cancer of the throat.

   The selection of the law officers was as delicate as the
partition of rôles in an amateur theatrical society. Every
judge on the list had influence; every one demanded the
right of presiding over the most famous case in French
criminal history. The judging in such an affair is not
empty celebrity; during its course the judge is the most
esteemed figure in society, for he has the allotment of the
court-tickets, one of which every great lady in the city
must secure. At last the claims, political, social, of Mr.
Counsellor Gilbert prevailed for the post of principal
judge: a very social eminence, a man of the world and

fashion, whose tact and appearance—his magnificent and well-groomed beard, his manicured gestures—hold some reminiscence of the great magistrates of Balzac. The less but still pretty office of Advocate-General, or prosecutor, was awarded to Maître Godefroy, a bearish determined fellow who was evidently making great progress in the 'career.' For Landru's defence the prize had long been taken: Maître Moro-Giafferi, a risen Corsican, with the largest and most profitable practice in France, as well as the assured commencement of a remarkable political career on one side or the other, had in the first month of Landru's success, seized it for himself, and was, long before the trial, in enjoyment of its luscious fruits of publicity.

So much preliminary drumming on the likelihood of enormous crowds at the opening of the case had the contrary effect: on the first day and until the truth was incautiously published by the reporters, the court was only moderately full. It was a hall the size of a meeting-house, distempered in a grim shade of green, whose only ornament was a huge gas-chandelier, gummy and long unused. The weather was cold, the light hard. In front of the judge's bench was a table covered with 'material evidence,' the heavier parts of which were stacked far into the body of the court, so that the witnesses on their way to the stand had to pick their way among the burst mattresses, the dismounted iron bedsteads, past a rusty stove, and look at the silky Gilbert across a square rod of false hair, cardboard boxes of bones, jewellery that all looked sham, books and iron bric-à-brac, the lesser spoils of Landru's victims. The front of the court thus had the sordid and depressing air of a house-removal. At the other end, there was a dock strongly barred off where throughout the trial the ticketless public stood in a slab: pale-faced rogues, gamboge-tressed women without hats, truant workmen, and inquisitive middle-class women from Paris, all day obsessed with the wish to gain a place nearer the front. In front of them were twenty rows of school benches, where the reporters of the world Press scribbled and quarrelled. On the third day the court changed: the whole of leisured Paris came to fight for places; a special train was run from the Gare d'Orsay in time for the opening. Both the cavernous corridors and the wet street outside were thick all day with a crowd that pushed like a panic to a theatre to get in. Gilbert's careful plans to admit only the flower of his friends were wrecked by force of numbers. The Sovereign People itself had come to enjoy the function of judging. A place inside, instead of being the present of a magistrate, was only to be won, like all the other privileges of a democracy, by competition, and became a trophy of ferocity in a woman, or cunning strength in a man. The successful part of the nation, once inside, consolidated positions, squeezed up beside the judge on his bench, forced its way beside the jurymen, and occupied every window ledge. The principle of representation was abandoned; Society moved itself to share in the condemnation and punishment of the offender. From this confined rabble at every significant point of the trial rose various sounds, ignoble roars of laughter, infamous grumblings, and yells of delight and excitement. It was never quiet. The ordinary machinery of justice clogged, only with the greatest hardship managed to enter into action at all. The jurymen took two hours and the assistance of a platoon of police to get to their box. The judge, though he had a private entrance, was often late. The reporters, unofficial delegates of our world civilization, abandoned their earlier composure in the crush and, fearing to be excluded from the function by which they earned their living, scuffled with the mob and fought their colleagues each for his own hand with no less determination.

The French dock is a long bench, raised to the same level as the judge's desk. In this, above the fleshly figure of his counsel, Moro-Giafferi, was the profile of Landru, russet and bleached bone. The horrible patina of the gaol was on his naked cranium, which seemed to shine in the wintry light from a window behind. His coat, which he never removed, was a mackintosh of the military cut fashionable when he was arrested: a shade lighter than his beard, which was trimmed in the shape of a fan. In the street he might have passed as one of those innumerable petty speculators that dealt in army stores. But on his dais framed by the broad blue gendarmes, with the aura of his iniquity, he seemed unlike any human seen before, as Napoleon might have appeared on the day of his anointing. His skull was certainly strange with its dead colour and incandescence. His nose was the greatest rarity, as thin and transparent at the bridge as a sheet of greased paper. When he sat and listened to the long requisitories, he could be taken for an actor in his carefully attentive pose, but so thin and delicate that one could notice the outline of the small, sharp elbow through his sleeve. We saw his full face but rarely: when he entered, stumbling and blinking through the side-door that ended

the stone stairs from the prison-yard every morning; and
sometimes when he turned to the roaring arena to protest.
Then we caught a glimpse of his cavernous eyes, which
never lost their abstraction even when he was shouting.
Usually his manner was chosen and finicky, but after a
few minutes in this style he would drop back into the
Paris twang. When Fernande Segret was giving her evidence he closed his eyes; once when the rough Attorney-
General, coming to the matter of Thérèse Marchadier's pet
dogs which were found strangled with a waxed thread
under an oleander clump at Gambais, rushed at him the
question: 'Is that how you killed all your victims, Landru?'—he seemed scared, and shook. Once, at eighth repetition of the question, 'What became of this woman,
Landru?' he lost his temper and stood up shaking his long,
large hands with rage. He had many poses. He seemed
sometimes like a fox, with his snout finding danger in the
air; sometimes he seemed false, sometimes he seemed like
a wood-insect, with undefined antennæ that felt their way
along the board in front of him. Sometimes he would
pause and slowly take out, wipe and don a pair of gilt
spectacles before an answer; then he seemed simply a prematurely old man. Usually he was obviously immersed in
a private dream; but he took great pleasure in the whirling
combats between the hairy prosecutor and his sleek Corsican defender. He had a weakness for minor details, on
which he extended himself, until he suddenly remembered
some warning he had had of the danger of these tactics
and sat down. The judge, after a few days' brow-beating,
treated him with consideration. Both of them were interested in the crowd: the judge stroking his beard with his

soft white hand, the accused sideways, without completely turning his head, as if he were eaves-dropping. As in all multiple murder trials, the evidence was largely a repetition, each new victim had been met in the same way, traced in the same way, perhaps killed in the same way, it may be by this abominable new weapon of a waxed thread round the neck while asleep, which no agonizing effort could disengage. Probably, too, Landru disposed of their bodies in the same way; like Pel and Soleillant dissecting them minutely, then burning the pieces to ashes in a red-hot stove, then no doubt by the aid of his motor-car strewing their few pounds of relics in the hedges of distant lanes. The witnesses stepped after each other monotonously; concierges in Sunday clothes, little old women with dingy reticules, dry-eyed sisters, moustached detectives with long and precise records of their failures. The crowd, subtly changing every day, ceased to pay any attention to these. It fed its thousand eyes on the figure in the dock, which grew lighter and more transparent every day, like a discarded carapace. Landru fell into somnolences that lasted hours, during which the heaps of papers in front of him had obviously no part in the reverie. The classic attitude of the mass-murderer towards his punishment. Maître Moro-Giafferi, who at first had difficulty in inducing his client to resign the first rôle to him, composed dramatic tantrums, revolved his black professional sleeves at the more honestly bad-tempered red advocate opposite, then, having had his effect, subsided, and put on pince-nez. The judge, badly handled by indignant reporters in the Press every morning, let an elegant melancholy creep over him, and little by little abandoned any effort to cow the crowd, which every day grew wilder and more primitive as the great moment of condemnation approached—and as the stage-element in its composition gradually gained the majority. Caricaturists, who in the first days had timidly made their sketches using their knees as easels, now boldly advanced among the undergrowth of *pièces de conviction,* blocking the defence's view of the witness-rail, and drew Landru to the life at three feet from his eyes. This seemed to please him and amuse him; at a sign from one of the artists he would turn his head at the angle they wanted. And a more encumbering breed, the Press photographers, doggedly impudent, lugged their ungainly apparatus into similar good positions and took time exposures of the court. To no avail—for the ration of winter light, already insufficient for their purpose, was now always barred off by the backs of those who had climbed into the window-ledges. Most photographers having failed, the camera-men took to the expedient of hanging incandescent lamps of great power over the prisoner's bench, when the court was not sitting, so that at any rate the great moment and the most interesting expression would not escape them and the millions for whom they deputized.

So the time arrived: the jury after all these days had nothing before them but a coincidence; but it was enough. Ten women (the prosecution fixed on this number somewhat arbitrarily) who had known, loved and followed Landru had vanished. In his possession were their papers, their birth certificates, their marriage papers, all the paraphernalia with which the human ant-hill tries to fix separate personality, without which there could be no emigration from France. Against this Moro-Giafferi could only weakly hint that possibly Landru had shipped them to the brothels of South America, where common super-stitition has it there come no newspapers. The man himself, in his extremity, had never dared to make such a defence. He relied on the weary romanticism of 'an honourable man will never tell a woman's secret,' which, carefully weighed by the stony jurymen, came to much the same thing. But to this the terrible quietus of the prosecution struck mortally: What? Women of over fifty? Women whose false hair, false teeth, false bosoms, as well as identity papers you, Landru, have kept, and we captured? The jury retired.

In these moments, while prisoner and judges were withdrawn, the court crowd, this assembly of a modern people which had just sacrificed 1,500,000 of its young men to preserve its institutions and its culture, was extraordinary. It had been waiting from an early hour to keep its place, and in its joy at success gave itself over to a debauch. These thousand compressed bodies were the elect of all Paris, all France, arrived by their abilities to the most coveted spectacle of the century: the sight of Landru's condemnation. They could not move, but within the inches of every one's power, they rioted with abandon. The shrill cries of women at the daring contacts of their neighbours, the screams, the high giggles of chorus girls, the shouts of rage or pleasure of the men, combined in a chorus. It filled the street outside, and filtered no doubt to the ears of the man waiting in the cold cell somewhere beneath, wrapping himself close in the warm quilt of his sentimental day-dreams. It was not the cold formula of a delegated justice, but the voice of outraged society itself, doing its own justice. A thousand incidents kept the crowd alive while the tedious jury kept it in waiting. Girls pulled by the legs tumbled from their perch in the windows, strong men forced themselves from three places distant upon each other and revenged their dignity on some enemy with blows, which falling generously on the people between were returned, or saluted with bellows of pain. At last the jury, ill at ease and silent, filed back and the door opened for Landru. Immediately there was a frenzy. As the man stood half bowed forward to catch his fate and his sentence, at precisely the right moment the photographers fired their illumination. There was a great glare of light over him. From every part of the massed hall arms protruded upward with black boxes, cameras which aimed at him. And as though in the throes of an eruption, figures shot themselves out of the crowd-level with hands waving and their faces distorted with the effort of their struggle. One man (according to some it was the dean of the Comédie Française) actually succeeded in leaping to one of the advocate's benches, and stood there, hilarious, with opera-glasses to his eyes, greedily scanning the lost criminal's expression.

When the court was empty, the servants found the floor strewn like a holiday beach with bitten sandwiches, papers, bottles, and other unmentionable, unmistakable traces of their presence which human beings, alas, must leave on a spot where they have been long hours kept immobile without privacy.

This immission of the sovereign people into judgment and punishment, or rather the disrespectful publicity given to it by the exasperated reporters, troubled the Government. They determined therefore that the final act, the execution of Landru, should be guarded, and only enjoyed by appointed proxies. Before dusk, troops took up their stations, and as soon as the trams stopped running, pickets enclosed the space of road outside the prison of Versailles, which is next door to the court. All the cafés and houses within this area were searched. Those numerous strangers, who, having shared or missed the condemnation, wished to witness the execution and had hidden themselves, sometimes in the most humble compartments of these places, were rigorously expelled beyond the barrier. Only the reporters were allowed to remain; these spent the night in billiards and dozing. Before dawn the guillotine was reared on the side-walk, before the principal door. At the appointed hour, before it was light, that door opened, and with tied feet, his chest bared by the executioner's shears, and ghastly rags of shirt hanging over his bound arms, Landru was jostled to the towering machine that in a flash ended him and all his secrets.

At that moment, by some error of the guards, a tram filled with workmen on their way to the yards was allowed to pass, and their curious crowded faces received the last sight of the living head of Desiré Landru.

The
Philanthropy
of
Fritz
Haarmann

Grans: Das kann man doch leichter bei Einem den man nicht liebt.
Haarman (belehrend):—Das is nicht richtig, Hans. Man macht das leichter, wenn man liebt.

.

Evidence at the trial.

CRIMINALITY IN GENERAL IS AN ALMOST IRRESISTIBLE subject for theory-construction, and the five mass-murderers we have examined have certainly enough in common for yet another exercise in that taste. Nor were they chosen with any of that sly premeditation by which Lombroso used to arrive at his mystifying conclusions; they are simply the worst, the most dangerous, the most wicked criminals of our century, the bottom of the vase. The verdict of whole peoples places them lower than any in the range, with the possible exception of Jack the Ripper—who for various reasons, of which lack of documentation is only one, was excluded from this study—Burke, Troppmann, Smith, Landru were more detestable than Palmer, Castaing, Pel, Pranzini, Cream, Pritchard, Avinain, Vacher, Voirbo, La Pommerais, Vandenlinden, Hélène Jegado, Schumann, or even than Holmes and Pierre Basson, to name but villains of the first magnitude during the century this civilization has lasted. So that from our four alone, with reasonable care, presentable inductions could be drawn, bearing not only on the whole criminal problem, but on the tactics and merits of the repressive organization of 'justice,' which is our reaction to it. It certainly is a temptation to follow up such clues as the early family discords all these worst men in differing degree, all had in their lives, more definitely even (except for the dubious case of Landru), their youthful hate of their fathers. Then there is that remarkable uniformity in their daily occupations, apart from their crimes, which I have already noticed. Even Troppmann, the only one with a specialized trade, showed signs that had he lived he would have abandoned this, and come into line. All, too, were men with some dealings with books and a taste for self-improvement. In their inner life, all were day-dreamers. All seemed not only to suffer but actively to cultivate a peculiar professional deformation, a point of view which in many ways bore a queer resemblance to that of men of the law and business. Each in their crimes obeyed the Law of Repetition. All were devoted family men; all, compared with their *milieu,* sober and methodical in their habits. The difficulty would not indeed be to find points of similarity. On the contrary, each of them so meticulously conformed to type that each might stand for the type in himself. And even a surface examination of all other mass-murderers of our century (excluding poisoners, who have their own queer laws) would, I dare say, show the same astonishing list of coincidences even to seemingly accidental features of their lives and methods.

The most sensational of all: that a respectable number of mass-murderers either stood before discovery on privileged terms with the police whose supreme task it should have been to kill them out, or had other quasi-legal protection, is true not only of Landru, who was certainly a police informer, and to this owed not only his long immunity from arrest, but the privileges of petrol and passes that allowed him to dispose of the bones of his victims; Burke, who was covered by the influence of Dr. Knox; Troppmann, whom Claude believed to have been an agent in the pay of one or both secret services in Alsace, but of a disquietingly large number of lesser multiple-murderers. Palmer of Rugeley had Ward the coroner in his pay. Prévost was a policeman. Voirbo was a political spy on the republicans in the pay of the Imperial Government. The subject of this last study, Haarmann, himself was a paid informer attached to the Hanover police. A still greater number had seen military service, or lived in times of warfever. Nevertheless, however tempting it would be to reunite all these characters and make a mass-murderer type distinguishable from the rest of humanity, even the rest of criminals by a score of specific characters, I am convinced that it would be a great stupidity. There is no mass-murderer type, any more than there is, except in the sinister jokings of a Lombroso, an *Uomo Delinquente*. The search for a species of man different from our law-abiding selves, *'simia homo sine cauda, pedibus posticiis ambulans, furax, inquietus cordis,'* which one day Society will learn to spot and hunt out, is vain. The scientist will never be able to give Society a useful *'portrait parlé'* of the race of Cain, men with 'projecting ears, thick hair and

thin beard, projecting frontal eminences, enormous jaws, a
square and projecting chin, large cheek bones and frequent gesticulation,' whom the police so armed can con-
veniently exterminate. The description fits too exactly, as a
French savant once remarked, with that of our own best
friends. And as he differs in no way in appearance from
the rest of mankind, so the mass-murderer is impossible to
distinguish by his ways of thought. It is true he fits the
mental categories of the paranoiac, and 'has as basic emotion, vanity, to which is added a strong element both of
acquisitiveness and avarice, moreover as regards character
persistent, opinionative and stubborn, is well versed in
legal procedure, in addition to the fundamental mark of
being ruled by passion and emotion rather than reasoning.'
But the description would also, in as many cases, fit the
judge who tries him, and the police-sergeant who arrests
him. The classic symptoms of paranoia, even *paranoia
querulans* that was possibly made specially to fit our mass-
murderer, are indeed an amazingly apt burlesque description of most civilized nations of earth, and of Society in
general as far as that is a real entity at all. The moralists,
of course, have always conceded this disdainfully about
the mob, the headless giant that browses and breeds in our
own times beside the higher organization of our own par-
liamentary, constitutional States, like a prehistoric monster survived its epoch; the mob that devoured Burke's
death, the mob that soaked itself in Troppmann's blood,
the mob that tried Landru. It is not so fashionable yet to
say the same hard things about that newest form of the
animal, that invisible mob whose circulation the giant

newspapers boast they direct, the 'public' which solemnly turned aside from the great killing over the water to watch the Brides in the Bath murderer have his neck twisted, though it may amply deserve it. But if anyone dared to remark it, the same diagnosis of paranoia fits far better the higher organism than the lower, the State-Nation itself, which would fare ill indeed before a courageous medical board of its own alienists, than the Mob itself. Who indeed is subtle enough to distinguish between the egotism of an individual and the patriotism of a nation? Or between private and national pride? There is no nation which does not claim to be stubborn, opinionative, persistent; no democracy that is not ruled by passion; no dictature that proceeds by reasoning. Nor is there any one, so far as I know, that does not boast of its system of legal procedure, which indeed is almost the only corporate enterprise, except war, in which nations have interested themselves seriously. And if those fantastic doctors, persisting in their humour, turned from their identification of the symptoms of our paranoiac commonwealths to an examination in the same taste of their acts, the jest would not wear itself out. What that the mob has done, what that our mass-murderers have done, that the State cannot outmatch? The poor mob indeed on such inquiry would turn out to be a harmless creature, guilty at most of from time to time an excusable *'crime passionel.'* Instead of a score or two of lynchings spread out over a century, any first-class State in the world could show as many killings every year, done on its own profession, not for hate or impulse, but for its cold and calculated self-interest. It is obvious that

Burke, Troppmann, Landru, Smith, and all their tribal brethren, were killed for the same reasons that they killed, for profit—the 'profit of the community at large,' of course, instead of that of one small individual. Nor can the circumstances of the deed in either case spoil much of the analogy. Burke was stifled, even as he stifled, Troppmann gashed even as he gashed. There is even credit taken for such not uncommon similarities, which are noted with pleasure, and the name of 'poetic justice' is applied to them by apologists of Capital Punishment. So in this interesting series the trial in court may be made to correspond, spitefully, with that painful pause before the act of killing, easy to discover in the life of the more wavering killer, any mass-murderer. I will not go farther in this impertinence, beyond a mere indication of the 'institution of war,' in which the best and noblest sentiments of nations are admittedly manifested. Where could a nation so miserable be found that it would not gladly use a thousand lives for a handkerchief of territory, or so poor-spirited as to see its commerce disappear without a fight for it? In this indeed, its supreme action, the State brushes aside all wounding comparisons; in the neighbourhood of a war, such as that last in which 12,000,000 perished, the mass-murderer loses all his claim to the wholesale, and becomes an infinitesimal wretch, engaged in minute wickedness unworthy of attention. So at the Landru trial, no lawyer dared to say that the prisoner made him shudder, or to lift the trial and condemnation of a man who had killed a mere thirteen out of the class of mere distractions. The honest Mob would have laughed him to scorn.

The reason why the correspondences we have ourselves noticed in the lives of mass-murderers are no more
valid for the construction of a class separate from the rest
of humanity than the symptoms and stigmata of the doctors is less amusing. The characteristics of these unspecialized men, with an ambition and culture, low as it is,
beyond the ruts of their surroundings, who have quarrelled
with their family, but nevertheless have a strong desire for
a family life of their own, these day-dreamers and Narcis-
sans, who substitute the most arid conception of law for
reality, these unsympathetics who magically attract sympathy, these cowards too frightened ever to change the
method of their first deed by a hair, yet undeterred by the
awful punishment that overhangs them; who run amuck
when their peril is greatest, and enjoy their own trials;
these eternal plotters who have no trace of imagination;
these experimenters in Sadism, who are sober, methodical
and over-thrifty, are apparently different and unconnected
with each other, but surely in their complete collection
they must mark a species of men apart? In reality, if rare
among the numerically insignificant possessing-classes of
modern States (which, because they alone have the power
to express themselves unduly, usurp for their own characters a sort of unthinking universality), not only are each
of these characteristics extremely common among those
lower classes which are in an overwhelming majority, but
their conjunction in one individual in certain regions of
those classes is as often met at least as any other form of
character. In fact, both externally and inwardly, both in
their ways and in their temperaments, such a breed is an

inevitable, if unintentional, by-product of the modern industrial society. Their manufacture may be explained almost mechanically. For if the industrial system be
simplified to its essentials, it plainly consists in a possess-
ing-class, and a reservoir of labour with an enormously
complicated network of intermediate channels connecting
the two. It is the interest of all except those forming it
that this basic reservoir, the working proletariat, should be
as large and as stable as possible. To this end various
devices have been evolved, on the one hand an infinity of
outlets, which we call vaguely 'the democratic chance,' by
which all individuals with force, originality or will may
ascend freely out of the mass, as far as their natural momentum will carry them, even to the high air of the
possessors themselves. This safety-valve system has been
found necessary everywhere because humanity in the
mass under pressure is highly explosive. Complementary
to it are a series of social forces, within the body of the
reservoir, of which the most obvious are the family and
the force of habit: ancient devices still useful in ordinary circumstances in keeping the reservoir in peaceful
cohesion. There is, further, built around the proletariat an
inflexible case or tank of laws, to prevent any molecule
flying off, except by the valves provided, or sinking as
sediment into a state of unproductive savagery beneath. A
further safeguard, that of religion, until the last generation very effective in some societies, seems to be losing
its efficacity everywhere. This, in its main lines simple,
system never, however, works perfectly. The reservoir,
because it is humanity and not a gas, is in perpetual com-
motion, naturally uncohesive, full of incalculable dis-

ruptive impulses. Even in normal times, force of habit is continually breaking down and setting particles free from their place; and the family tie, that relic of a freer epoch, is an undependable link in the immensely artificial slums of modern industrialism. So every year unnumbered men escape from the receptacle, against the will and interest of society, some physically and mentally weak falling in spite of the meshes of repressive law and philanthropy from a mode of life too hard for them to the sediment that is called the criminal class. Others defying the regulations of the democratic valves squeeze upwards to an easier life than their education or endowments entitle them to. It is these latter runaways, who have broken the family tie and escaped the law of monotonous labour which habit held them to, and forced themselves into the more leisured regions of trade above, that form that large class of unspecialized, sharp individuals to which, along with a tremendous majority of persons inoffensive to the life of their fellow-creatures, our mass-murderers clearly belong. Their only science is a very precise one of the holes in that mesh of law that could not confine them to the function which society appointed for them. Their only ideal is to follow remorselessly the bright vague light far above them that shines down from the heaven of possession. This is in ordinary times. But when the whole State, rich and poor, reservoir and pinnacle, is shaken by a war, or by some other calamity external to it, this process of dissolution within the reservoir and escape from its meshes is enormously increased: the social leakage is then very serious, and the vast intermediate world between the extremes becomes clogged with an innumerable crowd of intrusive bodies, most of them thrown up from below, some even shaken down from above, and then the feverish, disordered state of a 'post-war society' is to be witnessed. There is a natural family-resemblance between these displaced particles, for their origin and history have been the same. The force which dislodged them is unspent, they are self-seeking, ambitious, obstinate, and the rest. Without falling into a hopeless determinationism, it is hard to find any quality or trick in them whose origin in their history and circumstances cannot be sufficiently seen. But free in the endless veins of the system, they have different fates, as the accident of their movements disposes. Not all parasites are dangerous or irritating, all follow the same physiological habit. All develop notable organs of prehension and all degenerate in the organs of sense. The vast majority of our small swindling, wit-living self-liberators find the body of society such a congenial *milieu* that they are strictly symbiotic and even commensal, as the jargon goes, like the fish *fierasfer* who live in the digestive tube of the sea-cucumber without doing it any harm. They are accepted by that huge animal, Society (itself strictly parasitic on the earth), and give it one of its most characteristic features. But a few, like Burke and Troppmann and Smith and Landru, whom an accident has not settled in a warm corner, keep perpetually on the move, every year more agitated, until they become toxic. And, illogically, being mere units in the vast class of unproductive human beings displaced in the industrial civilization, which ranges from confidence men to the confines of the intelligent trader, they are then branded as a breed, not only separate from their fellow-shysters, but from the whole of timid humanity itself. Unjustly, because so rigorous an exile cannot be founded on an accident of adjustment. No one can nowadays dare to reproach such men, after a collective killing of such magnitude as we have all committed, of an exclusive mark of blood-stain. All our foreheads are smeared. Those who innocently persist in imagining that mass-murderers are different from themselves simply in that they had the awful courage to kill and repeat their act, a faculty in which they are to have some gloomy monopoly among the sons of men, I refer to the printed achievements of the heroes of the war; or if they are unwilling to read them again, I call the witness of all ex-combatants that at the Front it was never found difficult to induce even the mildest recruit to *kill*. Mere aptitude for homicide, even with the most ugly weapon, cannot divide us from these men, for we all most horribly and certainly possess it. Rather admire that these and not us, by the wave of living, are thrown in such a situation that it seems their direct interest to take another's life.

Without such an appeal to a sense of proportion and invitation to intellectual exercise, I would not dare to enter the case of Fritz Haarmann: without which, however, this series of mass-murderers would lack its capital. For in him, the ogre of Hanover, who was decapitated at the beginning of 1925, there are combined characteristics of all the rest, and his is the sum of all their guilt. Haarmann was possessed by the ghoul of Burke, and the wild beast of Troppmann. He bettered the satanic economies of Smith; and was damned in deeper erotics than Landru. Without any standard of measurement, this man was the chief murderer, the worst man, the last of the human race.

His case, singularly illuminating as it is, suffers from
two drawbacks. For the one, that he had once been confined in a lunatic asylum, and so might appear to belong
to those optimists who hold that madness is a sufficient
explanation of all crime, it is enough to recall that the
Hanover Court of Justice—supported fully by the 'gutach-
tungen' of its experts, Schultze, Professor of Psychiatry at
the University of Göttingen, and Dr. Alex Schackwitz,
Gerichtsmedizinalrat at Hanover, decided that Haarmann
could not benefit by the clause 51 St.G. B. of the German
Code: that is, was fully responsible for his acts. There
was also there produced a great wallet of earlier expert
opinions, dating from all salient points in Haarmann's
career, to the same effect. And, for what it is worth, there
are his own vehement protestations of sanity, which he
supported by a most reasonable bearing during the trial
and an impressive confession. Whatever the value of these
opinions, they are enough for permission to try to follow
this man in the spirit in which we have done the rest. The
second disadvantage is graver, I hope not insuperable; it
is that his motives were such that thirty years ago no
English book not intended for the doctors would have
dared allude to them: in fact, he was a homosexual and
killed (on his own confession, which I partly accept) in
paroxysms of erotic frenzy, though the profit he invariably
drew from his victims brings him fully into our scope.
Had this been a mere incidental in his crimes, it might
squeamishly have been omitted, or only hinted at in the
conventional way. But such treatment would stultify our
whole inquiry, by leaving one of its most profound mysteries unexamined, that of the evil pleasure which we have

so often suspected clustered about the primitive act of killing itself. In at least two of our instances, the killing of Mary Patterson by Burke, and that of the penniless girl, Babelay, by Landru, there were undoubtedly circumstances to hint that these acts, at any rate, were committed not entirely with extraneous profit in mind. For the beautiful Mary Patterson was not only out of the run of Burke's victims by her youth, but her hunting down had many unusual difficulties and dangers, and so stands by itself in his record of easier atrocities. So with the young Babelay: unlike all the rest of Landru's murders, hers brought him no money, and he could never have imagined that it would bring him money. These, there is a suspicion, were murders for more than profit. May not the avowals of Haarmann reveal a part of the redoubtable secret of the killer's mind, undetectable in any less formidable series: that killing may be accompanied by feelings of pleasure of a certain kind, not as one might a priori suppose, of those of the hate class of emotion, but of admiration, of desire? Of this Professor Theodor Lessing penetratingly remarks: 'We do not even know if, when animals tear each other to pieces, they do not experience a certain sensual pleasure, so that when the wolf strangles the lamb, one can say equally well, "he loves lambs" as that "he hates lambs." ' And following him still, quote the deep words, of Nietzsche. 'Thus said the Red Judge: Why doth this criminal kill? because he would rob? But I say unto you, his soul wished Blood not Robbery; he thirsted after the pleasure of the knife.' If this surmise be true, then there may be lurking for every murderer for profit in his first crime the deadly enticement to do another, and to so continue until the end of the tether, drawn on by an awakened devil for all time. Not to lose our heads, a perfect analogy for the militarism of nations in the lonely struggles of such individuals.

All that was known of Haarmann's life before he was arrested needs only a few lines. He was born in Hanover on the 25th October 1879. The son of a locomotive-stoker, who quit work, when his youngest son was five years old, to live on his wife's little fortune. The father, 'Olle Haarmann,' was a well-known character, a bad-tempered, grumbling, incredibly mean, everlastingly discontented man. The mother, seven years older than her husband, was a withered, prematurely-aged, silent woman, who had become bedridden after the birth of her sixth child, the future mass-murderer. She was then forty-one years old. One of the other children, Wilhelm, was sent to a reformatory for an offence against the twelve-year-old daughter of a neighbour. The three Haarmann daughters were all of unchaste reputation at an early age. The remaining son, the eldest, turned out a hard-working, small-minded, respectable foreman. We have here a group with neither cohesion nor stability, which the possession of a small property releases from the steady mass of the proletariat.

Fritz the youngest, the future murderer, almost as soon as he could walk, developed two suggestive characteristics: he loved dressing up and playing at being a girl, and he showed a deep enmity to his father. He loved dolls, and sewing, was never happier than when helping his sisters in the housework; he was bashful and frightened in the company of boys. At first he was sent to a Church school then, at the age of sixteen, to a preparatory school for non-commissioned officers at Neu Breisach. At that time he was a well-developed, healthy-looking boy, rather fat, with a regular, almost handsome face. He was a poor scholar, but a good soldier; on the 3rd September 1895, he was put in the military hospital, after a sort of fit, that he explained as sunstroke suffered during manœuvres. Later he was released from military service on this ground and at his own request. He returned home, and his father tried to put him to work in his own small cigar factory which he had started in 1888. Soon the seventeen-year-old Haarmann was accused of offences against children; he was sent to the Provincial Asylum of Hildesheim, being judged irresponsible for his acts; Dr. Schmalfuss, who examined him, considered him incurably feeble-minded. Whether part of this verdict is to be explained by his undoubted talent and propensity for 'simulation' in order to escape worse punishment, Haarmann expressed ever afterwards a great and apparently sincere horror of lunatic asylums. At his trial the phrase, 'Cut off my head, but do not send me back to the madhouse,' was always on his lips, possibly sincerely. It is said that, in his later years of freedom, the threat by one of his companions 'to send him back' was always sufficient to cow him. Six months later, on Christmas Day, while the asylum Christmas tree was alight, he managed to escape, and fled to Switzerland. Here he worked, first with a boat-maker, then with an apothecary in Zurich. After two years he returned to Hanover. Violent scenes between father and son, often

ending in blows, were common. Young Haarmann became engaged to marry, but broke it off. A child was
stillborn. Then he enlisted in the army as substitute, and
was sent to the crack 10th Jäger Battalion, in Colmar in
Alsace. He seemed to have found his proper place at last.
His officers were enchanted with him, one captain so much
so that he took him as batman. Like Burke and Landru
he was an ideal soldier, obedient, full of esprit de corps,
delighting in every insipid detail of the life. These years
he declared were the happiest of his life. They were ended
by another illness, diagnosed as neurasthenia, and he was
again released, with the character 'Recht gut' and a pension, which he drew until his final arrest in 1924, in spite
of many intervening convictions. On his return home
quarrels broke out again. His father summoned him for
violence and threats, and succeeded in having him medi-
cally examined once more. The expert, Dr. Andrae, made
his report on 14th May 1903. It gave as his opinion that
Fritz Haarmann was morally lacking, unintelligent, rough,
easily amused, revengeful, and entirely selfish, but not in
any proper sense 'mentally ill, so that there are no grounds
for sending him to a lunatic asylum.' Haarmann finally invested with this responsibility passed a third of the next
twenty years in prison, on various charges, ranging
from petty theft to burglary, fraud and indecency. The
forces, internal and external, acting on him during this
period may be summarized: the gravitation of society,
ever seeking to sink him to that stratum at the bottom
where he could be used, acting both negatively by its
economic law, which everlastingly tends to return small

possessors to the proletariat from which luck or thrift has momentarily freed them, and positively, by supplying him with a tolerable life there, in this case a military career which well suited him, and his unskilled employments in Switzerland. This compression Haarmann evades by his illness—whatever it was. Society retorts in three contradictory ways: first it locks him in an asylum, then it gives him a pension; then both banishment and bribery alike having failed to keep this wandering atom in its place, and stop it from its itching parasitism which rapidly develops—as if in bad temper the State sends him repeatedly to the torture of cellular confinement. The proper interpretation of the medical reports which decorate this period of his life is that the State was unwilling to content itself with the simple removal of an irritating parasite to the safe keeping of an asylum, but must also scratch. It indulges itself with a revengeful assertion of his responsibility, in order not only to segregate but to punish. This attitude, even to its own hurt, Society henceforward holds towards our subject, with occasional breaks, until the end of his pre-war period.

Besides these somewhat distracted direct actions on him, Haarmann naturally was also acted upon by the State's deputy—the family. His father's character has already been sketched. As his creation grew, this 'Olle Haarmann' grew into a fear of him, which showed itself in its customary guise of violent anger and hatred. This Halbert and Hob status was diversified by two attempts of the old man to anchor his son to his own calling, the first, to get him to work in the little cigar factory which ended by

Fritz showing such incompetence and dishonesty that it
had to be discarded; the second, by a just as hopeless purchase of a fried-fish business for him, which Fritz ruined
in a short time by his own depredations. The trading instinct indeed was highly developed in the young man, but
not at all that of keeping a stock. He could be trusted to
haggle and finesse, but he could not keep his fingers off
any property, even his own. With this venture the father
ceased dealings with his son, except for that last desperate
attempt to get him confined in a lunatic asylum. The rest
of the children, at any rate the women, kept some sort of
a habitual relationship to the scapegrace, which might
stretch to a meal and a bed for one night, but hardly more.

So the finished product was loosed on the world to
follow his own internal impulses, disastrously modified
by all the influences he had received. The State had used
all its best tools upon him: church, prison, army, school,
family, asylum—it can hardly disclaim direct responsibility
for the result. Like the rest of our examples, this mass-
murderer in the making has come out of this extraordinary tutoring rather an unenviable fellow, but there are
signs of a natural good nature not entirely eradicated. The
prevailing tint of gloom in the others may have been
caused by some speck of conventional morals in them that
had turned sour; Haarmann, who is chemically pure of any
such thing, is often gay, sometimes generous, usually sentimental: hardly ever introspective. His fruitless hatred for
his father seemed to have absorbed most of his capacity
for active enmity; he is a vagabond hawker, a mumping
pedlar, clothes-thief, unspecialized pilferer and occasional

burglar, popular amongst fellow-thieves, and even among the police, who reckoned him as one of the sensible lags who come quietly when touched on the sleeve. His sexual abnormality scarcely sufficed to mark him out to them from the nondescript mass of his likes; if we may trust Havelock Ellis, there is always a high proportion of such persons among tramps, 'spielers' and the like. In any case, the town of Hanover has always been notorious in Europe for the prevalence of Haarmann's vice. In 1918 indeed, in this middle-sized town of only 450,000 inhabitants, there were 500 'männliche Prostituierten' inscribed on the police lists, and no less officially the Chief Criminal Inspector estimated the total number of homosexuals there as about 40,000: that is proportionally if not actually much greater than in Paris. To the police, then, during these twenty years of his manhood, as well as to his fellows, Haarmann was nothing but a stoutish, almost inoffensive 'hobo' differing from thousands of other refractory subjects of the State's rearing by nothing bad—rather, indeed, by his good-nature, his waggishness, his sometimes humorous incorrigibility. Just before the outbreak of the war, he was sentenced to his longest sentence for an extensive series of thefts and frauds from a warehouse where he had been employed—five years. So this 'born soldier,' as the Jäger officers did not hesitate to call him, even afterwards, passed the whole of the war in the enforced peace of a prison.

He was released in 1918, to perhaps the most curious experience a man could have: the sudden, unprepared spectacle of all that Germany had done to herself in five heroic years. An imaginative man might have been frightened at the contrast: Haarmann felt the surprise indeed, but pleasurably. The sight of the new times sent him into a fit of solitary laughter. Into this new world he had to adjust himself, as he had adjusted himself to the less obviously amusing world of the pre-war; the job seemed to him immensely easier. For a hurried look round Berlin, where the crowd was standing ten deep and half a mile long before the bakeries, followed by a return to native Hanover on a train where a ticket cost a crazy fortune, but where there were no ticket collectors, showed him that at last Society, tired of trying to convert its Haarmanns, had resolved to imitate them. Everywhere he saw the swindler and the huckster installed; the last laugh raised in judgment against the honest and industrious; the whole world turned go-between; and the competition did not frighten him. He has summed up his first impressions with a very natural art: 'When I was let out of "Kitchen," I went to Berlin. There was not much up. I came back to Hanover. And so, to sister Emma's. Bertchen, her youngest, says to me, "Don't eat so much bread, uncle. We have to 'snake up' for it; we're all ill." Says I, "I'll go and have a look, kid, what's to be done." So then I went to the Railway Station. Emma gave some cash. Talk about profiteers and hagglers! (Schieber und Hamsterer.) That's where they were, indeed. We had a good talk; I got everything there. We all got fat again with what I got.'

In fact there was not a much better town in Germany to observe the new mode of life than this Hanover, and the centre of Hanover was at the Head Railway Station and the square outside. For Hanover, because of its balanced geographic situation, four train hours from Berlin where a host of reluctant republicans were scrambling for power, and eight hours from Cologne where the British Army were freely circulating the only sound money in the country, had opened an episode unique, even in its eccentric history, as the chief 'schieber' market in Germany: at a time when the very Reichsbank itself was 'schieber.' This trade, in whose nature there was something of thieves-market, something of smuggling, something of a huge process of pawnbroking for a whole era, short in counted years, long in misery, virtually supplanted all other forms of commerce. Outside it was the card system, stupid, proud, honest, by which all honest, proud or stupid men were doomed to slow starvation, to death. The only way to obtain meat, bread, milk enough to keep body and soul alive was Haarmann's way—opposite the Railway Station, in the Schieber market. Here at thousands of little stalls were sold daily from under board to under coat tails all the stolen, smuggled, swindled meat, from veal and ducks and geese, to dogs and cats, and other even more forbidden flesh, as will later appear from Haarmann's story, with all the other necessities of our civilization, boots, cigarettes, chocolates, margarine, and all varieties of second-hand goods. Looking down asquint on this square alive with hagglers was the sham Gothic bulk of the Railway Station itself: another focus of the new life. For here in the huge waiting-halls, over their pavements littered with the refuse of a crowd that never dissolved, was the head-quarters of the floating population, the homeless, the wanderers, the fugitive, the workless. In the day they used it for a base. In the night they shared the heat of its stoves. Runaway boys from the farthest towns of North Germany, workless labourers from the factories closed by the English embargo, out-of-heel professors, sneak-thieves who had their stalls in the square outside, and later poor devils of patriotic refugees from the occupied regions of the west, tramped irregular courses from one ever-swinging portal to the other, for hours and days there, and at night they slept wedged together on the sticky benches to eke out the temperature with the animal warmth of their bodies. Haarmann, still glowing with the excitement of finding the market outside, found in this rendezvous his heaven of good company.

So, suddenly transported as if by a fairy's wand into a *milieu* perfectly suited to his talents, tastes, and habits, Haarmann started to develop luxuriantly. He put on weight, as he says, like a stray dog adopted by a butcher, and he lost his slink. In six months he had found a dwelling, in Cellarstrasse 27 in the old quarter of the town; he had started a business of meat-hawker which prospered; he had found a place as police-spy, or informer; and he had committed his first murder. These things hung together, as do the acts of any well-co-ordinated life. I agree with Lessing that the fundamental that conditioned the success of all the others was his relation with the police. The causes of it were simple and necessary. By the decision of the Allies, itself caused and excused by the behaviour of the German State in the war, more than a million people were starving to death. There was revolution and counter-revolution, and very complex ruin. The incompetent and dishonest authorities sought to perform

the primary and ineluctable task of all States—to keep the
people quiet—by an intensive system of police spying.
The regular police organizations, even if they could have
kept out of reach of the universal demoralization, were
too few. In Hanover, in the section charged with *moeurs,*
there were only twelve constables and detectives to deal
with over 4,000 registered prostitutes, as well as the
500 male prostitutes already mentioned. The police were
shamefully underpaid, so much so that they often became,
at the end of the 'hungry time,' grateful and dependent on
the smallest tips in kind, meat, bread, etc.: even from the
criminals they had to arrest. The tide of the new lawless-
ness became so colossal that, without the help of sneaks
and informers, paid with immunities (for there was no
money in the police chest), there would not have remained even the pretence of any guarantee to property
and life. The effects of generations of State organization
and education of the people by church, school, prison,
were being brutally tested; in that supreme examination, it
appeared that their permanent influence for good—in
which so many well-meaning energies had been spent—
was hard to find. Once the training stick was pulled up,
the tree sprawled as if it had never been tied. To keep
even a semblance of order, and even to save their own
lives from revenge, the hungry, impotent survivors of the
once massive organization of the police were obliged to
make friends with such helpers as they could find, the persons whom English slang used to call 'narks,' for whom
the Germans have a variety of names: *Spitzel, Zuträger,
Actgroschenjungen, Provokateur.* The gross Haarmann's

offer to serve as one of these was accepted: even eagerly accepted.

With this advantage the last bar to Haarmann's full
self-expression had gone. He could now exhibit without
restraint what the State's painstaking education had made
of him. In the first place, he was thoroughly trained for
the new life his master now generously spread before him.
The police cherished their new colleague, who had a vast
and intimate knowledge of the things they wished to hear,
the plots that were preparing against property and the
Government, the whereabouts of men they wished to lay
hands on, and no scruple hindered Haarmann from serving them against his own friends. Also, Haarmann made a
success of his 'N.E.P.' business in meat, far more than his
father had ever been able to do with cigars. With amazing
skill, he undersold his competitors, and he always—more
difficult—had goods to sell. The housewives round the old
quarter got to know this round-faced, high-voiced vendor,
who added something solid to his illicit traffic by his title
of 'Detective Haarmann.' In the railway waiting-rooms,
his stocky yet pliable form grew to be known and respected as on the Schieber Market. None of the regular
railway police, with whom his position put him on good
terms, were so diligent in their curiosity about new-comers
to the dormitory, or so wisely philanthropic in their dealings with that most difficult element, the runaway workless
boys. A rumour grew that Detective Haarmann represented the 'Midnight Mission.' Every day arrived a new
detachment of these youngsters of the war-generation.
They stepped out, covered in coal-dust, from goods-wagons
where they had ridden hundreds of miles without a ticket;

they crawled from under the axles of expresses sometimes, and very often they arrived on foot, limping and pale, from the villages within a hundred miles round. They had left home, because their fathers were dead in the war, and there was not food at home, or sometimes because their fathers had returned safe from the war, and there were two masters in the house. Flotsam and Jetsam of the Family, which like all its other possessions, material and ideal, the State had sold up in its bankruptcy.

Haarmann made a specialty of these boys. At three in the morning the man would come into the hall, and walk round slowly and seriously, with that air of authority that is so easy to learn by a newly-made official, scrutinizing all, appraising all; picking out some snoring youngster in a corner, shaking him, asking for his ticket, listening to his snivelling story gravely. Then, his round face relaxed in a peculiar smile, he would offer a mattress and a meal in his own rooms in the town.

The first to follow this benevolent man was Friedel Rothe. Haarmann was found guilty of exactly twenty-four murders; he himself made the estimate 'Es können dreizig, es können vierzig sein; ich weiss das nicht'—thirty or forty, he didn't remember. It would be impossible to give particulars of the majority. Friedel Rothe must stand as a general portrait of them all; their family likeness is unmistakable. Rothe was born in 1901, he disappeared on the 27th September 1918, in the full 'Elendszeit' when the Germans had nothing to eat. His father, Oswald Rothe, was at the Front. His mother could do nothing with the wild young Friedel. He was preparing for the elementary school examinations, but he would not work and spent his

time at street-corners, smoking, betting, yarning with his
friends. He secretly took his father's civilian clothes and
sold them to get money: that evening he did not come
back home. Next day he was seen at a distance by a
friend of the family, going round a corner near the 'Schieber Market.' After two days his mother received a post-
card from him: 'Dear Mother,—It's more than two days
since I ran away. But I will only come home if you promise to be nice to me. Affectionate greetings, your son,
Fritz.' The same day, the father returned from the war.
Both parents immediately started to search for the lad.
Several of Friedel's friends had something to reveal. One,
the fourteen-year-old Jewish boy, Paul Montag, a handsome creature with cold blue eyes, specially. He said that
Friedel had scraped acquaintance with a 'fine gentleman,'
a detective, who had given him presents and taken him
for a ride in the park. Friedel had met this man repeatedly. He had confided to Montag, 'I have been to his
room; there we smoke and amuse ourselves.' With this
clue the parents renewed the search and finally arrived at
Cellarstrasse *27*, Haarmann's lodging. With an infinity of
trouble, almost by force, they made the police search the
premises. Haarmann was found with another boy in such
circumstances that his colleagues were obliged to arrest
him, and he received nine months' imprisonment for indecency. But they searched the room so perfunctorily that
they found no trace of the missing boy. Four years afterwards, Haarmann in his cell, awaiting trial for twenty-four
murders remarked: 'At that time when the policeman arrested me, the head of the boy Friedel was hidden under

a newspaper behind the oven. Later on, I threw it into the canal.'

This interlude of imprisonment seems to have stopped his connection with the room in the Cellarstrasse. In 1919 (September) he found another place, in the Nikelaasstrasse; his landlady objected to his visitors and his ways, and then he moved farther along in the same street. It was at this new address that he first met his adored friend, the young Hans Grans, whose destiny is henceforward inseparably united with Haarmann. Grans was a muscular youth with a girlish face and a graceful walk: in another sphere of life he might have become by temperament and looks one of those undetermined young men, half professional dancer, half cicisbeo, who have made a new demimonde in the palace hotels at the health-resorts. Grans was abnormally idle, vain and predatory, with egotism which, but for his lack of energy, might have entitled him to a fore front place among criminals for himself. In the sphere of life to which God had called him, as the Catechism injuriously puts it, he did what he could, he was *maquereau*, petty thief, informer, bully, urning, and Haarmann loved him at sight. It is noticeable that once the two were together their acquaintances considered Grans infinitely the greater scoundrel, though twenty-four years of age and practice separated them. Even at the trial, after Haarmann's hair-raising confession had been read, the jury, the public, the judges all obviously felt more repulsion for the good-looking boy than for his terrible and unprepossessing companion. Haarmann was only a parasite on society, but Grans was a parasite on Haarmann, the sucker of his gains, the profiteer of his profiteering, the reason for his horrible efforts. Haarmann stubbornly accused Grans, in addition, of having been the direct instigator of his murders, of whose every detail he was pre-aware; also of having with another youth of the same style —one Wittkewski—committed at least two murders on his own account. Professor Lessing, however, considers that this charge was false; that it was due to Haarmann's jealousy of Grans, and part of a cunning plot for revenge: a judgment from such an observer who knew both accused intimately must be accepted. Grans undoubtedly belonged to a higher class in society than Haarmann, he had attended a High School; his parents kept a small lending library in the darkest corner of the old town. All efforts to make him work at a trade having failed, Grans left his home and joined the under-life of Hanover.

This under-life is the music to which the fable is set. There are some provincial cities which the contractile centralization of all government into capital cities, a chief feature of the nineteenth century in Europe, still leaves a distinct life of their own. France has two or three such cities, Germany more, but there is none in which the difference that survives is more curious than this Lower Saxon Hanover. The astonishing fortunes of its ruling family have left little trace beyond the material bulk of the high Welfenschloss, the never-dwelt-in palace of the Guelphs. Something that was there long before Elector George Louis left to take up the greatest legacy in Europe has survived the imperial annexation of the Prussians and the overwhelming factory population they brought with them, something that still marks fatally this city, more than any of its prosaic merits: the mysterious curse of an estrangement from nature that has entered deep into the personality of the city. How deep, it needed the terror of Haarmann to reveal. The roots of Hanover's old secret must be somewhere in the old-town quarter, undiscoverably hidden among the tangle of roofs where even the sparrows might lose their way. Dormer looks at attic across deep courts, where the old women store their boxes; cracked towers signal to innumerable chimneys which have never ceased reeking for five hundred years. Deep incrustations of soot and the rotting of the weather have set a patina on all the walls of these corrupt ancient places, more beautiful and more poisonous than copper. Behind them, there are innumerable corners and doorways, from which stiffen staircases, some with noble carvings of stone, some as perilous as the ladders to a barn. These lead to crowded rooms behind, ancient flagged halls of merchant-princes; obscure cubbyholes which have never had a window, which with the flagged courtyards below, the leprous slopes of the thousand roofs, the streets where two men could not pass abreast and with a blind corner in ambush every twenty yards down to the thick black ooze of the river Leine, are the haunts and sleeping-places of children and men, traitor cats and mangy dogs, cage-linnets and washer-women and the brown rats in the day; and in the night, of shadows. Though it is old, this 'Ghost-quarter' is never still from roof top to cellar, from the streets, where there are always children, to the very depth of its walls, where behind the crumbling wainscoting there are always rustlings and creepings; signs of a hinter-life in the crevices, that breeds and infests this uncleansable world. Here were Haarmann's homes, first in the Cellar-strasse on its borders, under the very wall of the new purple brick Prison; then with Hans Grans in the Neue Strasse; and afterwards, like a disease that works towards the heart, in the very centre of it all, the Rothe Reihe, the Red Row, the old Ghetto main-alley under the walls of the Synagogue. But each of his lodgings was the gateway to an even greater mystery than the labyrinth of the old town.

If the antique curse of Hanover certainly has its secret roots in this region it has also its flowers of peculiar sterile charm, which seduce thousands like young Grans from the insipidity of family and work. In the Georgstrasse, the thoroughfare of New Hanover itself among the broad gardens and rows of lime-trees, was the centre of the special society of Hanover, the Café Kröpcke: in 1918 the known market or gathering-place of faded, perfumed boys like Grans, where they met their clientele. Kröpcke was the entry to a peculiar little world of its own, with its own usages, meeting-places, manners. Here in the days of Grans and Haarmann could be had invitations to the balls in the Kalenberger Vorstadt, where in the finest hall of the city men danced all night with youngsters dressed in travesty. There was another such rendezvous in the old Assembly Rooms. This world had its own castes, or more properly, moods; for the lowest of these was set apart the tiny dancing-place called 'Zur schwülen Guste'—to give slang for slang, 'At Hot-Stuff Gussie's,' to which a section of these people were particularly devoted, And beyond and below all these centres there were the rambling warrens of

the Old Town itself, Little Venice, Red Row, the old
Ghetto, and the rest, the breeding regions of the very
poor, from which somewhere in the recesses of history the
poisonous growth took its beginning. All of these rendezvous Grans and Haarmann knew, from the gay and flash-
ing Kröpcke to the tenebrous mysteries of the Old Town.
The couple were a part of its spectacle, the coarse clown-
ish man, whose equivocal gestures and his voice contrasted
significantly with his bulk, and the clear-cut icy boy who
was his lord and master.

In the Cellarstrasse, where Rothe was last seen, Haarmann was active in his trade of 'gehamstertes Fleisch,'
smuggled-meat vendor. There was a constant succession
of boys carrying carefully closed parcels, which they left
with him, and most nights the neighbours heard through
the thin partition the noise of chopping. One woman,
Frau Seemann, who lived under Haarmann's workshop, a
greedy, curious, timorous woman, once knocked on her
ceiling while the man was at work and called out: 'Am I
going to get a bit?' The high effeminate voice answered
at once: 'No, next time.' One day he brought her a sack of
bones. 'I made soup of them, but I thought the bones
were too white so I threw it away.' The odious suspicion
of cannibalism that hung over the Haarmann case, though
it was certainly never proved, must be reckoned with. If it
had been without parallel in the times, we might brush
aside the universal belief of the Hanover populace that
Haarmann had been guilty of this last monstrous exploitation of his victims, the piecemeal sale of their bodies, and
accept with relief the frantical efforts of his prosecutors

to disprove it. But before the first frightened whispers against the Hanover ogre began to run, there was a partially proved case in Berlin, hurriedly ended by the sequestration of the accused man in a lunatic asylum; and while Haarmann was still standing his trial, the abominable discovery of one Denke in Münsterberg (December 1924), a quiet farmer known to the whole region as Papa Denke, whose guilt in a vast number of crimes similar to those of which Haarmann was suspected, was terribly certain. Here again the shame was partially covered by the apt suicide of Denke: not before, however, his discovery had caused the strangest scenes of collective hysteria among his miserable ex-customers. In Germany at any rate, socially the most advanced State in our civilization, the war series, from the band music to man-eating was thus actually completed. In four years action of the State, guided by statesmen whom it would only be a paradox to call criminals, in the strict observance of the most banal political morality, the days of werewolves and anthropophagi were brought back in Europe.

Whether Haarmann drew this last profit from his victims, whether Grans knew of it and urged him to it are matters which will now never be known for certain. But that Grans drew profit (and perhaps the main profit) from his companion's exploitation of the possessions of the murdered boys is tolerably sure. The method of trapping was usually the same as that followed in the first case of Rothe: Haarmann, often accompanied by Grans, would go to the Railway Station at night, and either using his authority as unofficial police-attaché, or sometimes through the more subtle intermediation of Grans, would fasten on a boy, take him away to his lodging, kill him in his own fashion, then hack up the body—either for further use, or as he rather unbelievably claims (in spite of careful dragging operations in the Leine complete skeletons were very rarely found) to throw into the river. Then he would hawk the clothing and such small possessions as the victims had on the thieves' market. When any garment took Grans' fancy, he would take it for himself. Haarmann always insisted that he was guided in his own selection of victims by liking; on two or three occasions he protested bitterly that the young jackal Grans had pushed him to murder when he hated the look of the proposed victim.

From 1918 to 1923 there is no exact evidence of his murders; these, in the opinion of all and on his own hinting confession, must have been numerous. After February 1923, we have the details of twenty-seven disappearances in which Haarmann was involved.

12th February 1923. Fritz Franke, 'the Berliner,' 17 years old. A pleasant red-haired fellow. He had stolen goods from his father's house and run away. His effects passed to Grans. A feature of this case is that two streetwomen, friends of Grans, visited Haarmann's room when both men were away, and poking about the cupboards came upon a great quantity of meat, whose look so aroused their suspicions that they took a sample to the police. The police expert made a report that it was nothing but pork. After this incident, which shows the prevailing feeling about Haarmann—though his popularity was still considerable—Haarmann continued in the police service. An inspector set up in business for himself as a private

detective under the name of 'The Lasso Agency' and took
Haarmann into partnership. From this connection he obtained a stamped pass which increased his prestige. He
may also at this period have been extensively used against
the Communists; this, like his situation as recruiter for the
Black Reichswehr, the patriotic association which with the
tacit encouragement of the authorities opposed the French
occupation of the Ruhr, cannot be proved. The conduct of
the trial later was such that it can give no confidence that
this negation implies very much. At any rate, Haarmaan
had throughout his last years a great fear of Communists,
so much so that he refused the offer of a celebrated Berlin
barrister, a specialist in the psychiatrical aspects of crime,
because he heard that he belonged to the extreme left wing
in politics. Both activities would have afforded the murderer obvious advantages in his dealings with his victims,
by promises and threats, and also a safe cover against any
inquiry into their fate.

20th March 1923. Wilhelm Schulze, 17 years old. An
office-boy who came to Hanover looking for work. Clothes
found in the possession of Haarmann's landlady.

23rd May 1923. Roland Huch, a strong boy of $15\frac{1}{2}$,
son of a chemist; ran away to go to sea. His parents made
strenuous efforts to trace him, but met with a cold recep-
tion by the Hanover police when they asked for inquiries
to be made in the neighbourhood of the Red Row. Clothing sold by Haarmann.

May 1923. Hans Sennenfeld, 20 years old. A shop-
keeper's son who fell into the bad company of *Schwülen
Guste*. His clothes were made into scouring rags by a
certain Gravorwilli, to whom Grans sold them.

25th June 1923. Ernst Ehrenberg, 13 years old. Son of a neighbour of Haarmann. Disappeared after a trip with the C.V.J.M. (Y.M.C.A.). A year later his green canvas knapsack was traced to the possession of Haarmann.

24th August 1923. Heinrich Struss. Eighteen years old. Worked in the suburbs, whereby he had each day to take the train. One night he did not return home. After Haarmann's arrest, small possessions of the boy were found in his possession, notably a key-ring which locked Heinrich's box, wardrobe and violin-box at home.

24th September 1923. Paul Bronischewski, from Bochum in the Ruhr, aged 17.

September 1923. Richard Graf. Aged 17. The youngest son of a family in Hanover managed by a 'little mother' of twenty.

12th October 1923. Wilhelm Erdner. Aged 16. Disappeared from work. The father met his son's friend 'Honnerbrock,' detective, who informed him that he had been forced to arrest his son for vagabondage. Inquiry at the police station showed that this name Honnerbrock was unknown, the father afterward identifying the man as Haarmann.

25th October 1923. Hermann Wolff. A loiterer on the Railway Station; boasted of his acquaintanceship with a detective. To the charge of having made away with him, Haarmann opposed one of his rare denials, which was accepted by the Court. He said: 'I have my tastes, after all. Such an ugly creature as, according to his photographs, your son must have been, I would never have taken to. You say that your boy had not even a shirt to his name.

And his socks were tied on to his feet with string. *Pfui Deibel*. You ought to have been ashamed to let him go about like that. Poor stuff like him there's plenty. Just think what you are saying. Such a youngster was much beneath my notice.'

27th October 1923. Heinz Brinkmann, aged 13. Lost at the Railway Station. During search for him, a friend came across Haarmann, who he learnt was a detective charged with the control of the waiting-rooms. Heinrich's clothes afterwards traced to the possession of Haarmann.

November 1923. Adolf Hannappel, aged 17. Dismissed from a milkman's farm for eating too much. This is one of the cases in which Haarmann accused Grans of having incited him to murder against his will, to have the new trousers of the boy, which Grans coveted.

6th December 1923. Adolf Hennies. Nothing of him has ever been found except his old overcoat, traced to Haarmann's possession. There was a serious quarrel over its possession, which almost ended in Grans separating from Haarmann.

17th May 1923. Hans Keimes, a handsome boy of 17. After reporting his disappearance, the Keimes family received a visit from Haarmann himself, who asked to see a photograph of the youth and promised if the youngster were in Hanover to find him within three days. The daughter was 'startled at his devilish laugh' when he said this. After this visit Haarmann denounced Grans as the murderer of the boy to the Police Station, but on Grans furnishing proof that he was actually under arrest for some minor offence at the time he was allowed to go. Nothing further of this case is known, beyond the finding of the body (unlike most of the rest), strangled and tied, in the canal.

5th January 1924. Ernst Spiecker. Seventeen years old. Had made Haarmann's acquaintance in the dance-hall, Schwülen Guste. Grans was wearing this boy's shirt when arrested.

15th January 1924. Heinrich Koch. An habitué of the special 'Bals Masqués.'

2nd February 1924. Willi Senger. Twenty years old. A 'Bahnhof Neper' (station loafer). His overcoat found in Haarmann's room.

8th February 1924. Hermann Speichert. Aged 15. An apprentice at the Power Station. He had said to friends: 'I don't like work any more. I have found a friend who is going to take me abroad.'

6th April 1924. Alfred Hogrefe. Seventeen years old. Played truant from his work. His parents threatened to punish him. He disappeared—to meet Haarmann.

April 1924. Hermann Bock. A young thief from the Railway Market. His friends knew that he had last been seen in Haarmann's company, and questioned him. Haarmann promised to take the matter up with the police and make inquiries. This case is a special one; Bock was older than Haarmann's other victims—twenty-three; a 'normal,' a rough fellow well able to take care of himself. This murder, which was strongly denied by Haarmann, seems to have been committed, if he were guilty, from motives of pure robbery. But the jury followed their practice, and as in the other case that Haarmann disputed (Wolff) acquitted him, though Bock's clothing was traced to him.

17th April 1924. Wilhelm Apel, aged 16. A dreamy,

romantic schoolboy. His father reproached him with cig-
arette-smoking; he did not come home.

26th April 1924. Robert Witzel. Aged 18. A frequenter
of the Café Kröpcke, behind the back of his parents. Last
seen in company of Haarmann. His skull, identified by its
teeth, was found in the Leine.

9th May 1924. Heinz Martin. Aged 16. His father was
killed at the war. Said he was going to sea, because his
mother made him make the beds. His clothes found in
Haarmann's room; Haarmann admitted the murder after
long denials.

26th May 1924. Fritz Wittig. This, and the Hannappel case were claimed by Haarmann to have been done on
the direct instigation, even command of Grans.

25th May 1924. Friedrich Abeling, a ten-year-old
child. Disappeared while playing truant. On the 17th June
a man came up to the children playing near the school he
had attended, and asked one of them: 'Do you know
Alice Abeling?' (the sister of the murdered boy). Alice
was there, and the man said to her: 'Good morning,
Alice. I have just come from your mother's house where I
left a card. Your mother will tell you all about me. I am a
friend of your father. I only wanted to see you.' He shook
hands and went away. There was no card at home, and
no knowledge of the man. Later Alice and her little friend
formally identified Haarmann as the man who had thus
strangely accosted them. It was afterwards established that
Haarmann had met Friedrich when he was loitering about,
afraid to go home, and had enticed him to the house in
the Red Row by a promise of sweets.

5th June 1924. Friedrich Koch. Aged 16. Another

youth who took train daily to his work. His leather lunch-
eon-bag, in which was written his name, was found among
Haarmann's effects.

14th June 1924. Erich de Vries. Seventeen years old.
Another whom Haarmann's presents of cigarettes lured
to his death.

It is no surprise, remembering not only Haarmann's
special relations with the police, but also the precedents of
other prime murderers, that his discovery and arrest is not
at all to be placed to the credit of society's paid guardians,
the police. The amuck period had long been passed by
the man. He killed more openly than Burke. In the Red
Row attic, where the walls were afterwards found to be
plastered with blood, not only did the thinness of the
partitions not trouble him, but on the mornings after a
murder, he would clean up as unsecretively as a lawful
butcher, and carry the bucket covered only by a towel
down the main stairs in full light of day, whistling and
greeting anyone he met. Remorse, so he says, sometimes
seized him, but never fear. Once he sat on the bed and
said tearfully to Grans: 'Hans, why am I different to other
men? Perhaps I have two souls.' But this, if it is true, was
only one of many maudlin moments, when he itched to
discuss himself like a *femme incomprise*. No emotion
stopped him from methodically collecting the clothes and
possessions of his victim and disposing of them, either in
presents to Grans or on the market. The lesser objects he
would often indeed give as a present or at a reduced rate
to his landlady or her friends. The suspicions of the two
women friends of Grans have been mentioned: one might
well ask if the deeds of Haarmann were not known and

accepted by those of his circle, not all of them by any means of the criminal class? The constant inquiries of bereaved parents, the occasional searches of Haarmann's lodging by his friends of the police; the comings not always followed by goings of strange boys, invariably followed by the chopping noises and the cleaning-up, and a new stock of second-hand clothing on the market: did this mean nothing to the neighbours, already, it would appear, quite willing to pass over an accusation of cannibalism? And this constant linking of Haarmann's name in police reports with the disappearance of boys, coupled with his known reputation of a man many times convicted for his dealings with them? Did this never arouse the horrified attention of the police chiefs and doctors? Apparently not. It was not until after his arrest that his neighbours and the guardians of the town showed even the slightest repulsion for him, or refused his company or his gifts. The organism had developed a toleration, through its fever, even for a Haarmann.

The accident occurred first. On the 17th May 1924, street urchins who were playing on the banks of the Leine near the castle found a human skull. On the 29th of the same month, farther down the bank another skull, small, apparently that of a boy, was found. On the 13th June, two more skulls were seen in the mud. All these finds were sent to the police doctor, who seemed to hold the theory that they were a joke of medical students. Or that they were washed down from Alfeld, where at the time there was a great plague of typhus. But on the 24th July, boys at play again came upon a horrible trove: a sack of whitened human bones, as well as another skull. This find frightened the people out of their indifference. A rumour arose like a wind from nowhere that: 'There is killing in the Old Town. Young children have been done away with in cellars. Boys have been drowned in the river.' It was commonly known that human flesh had been sold on the Station Market. And a story of a 'werewolf' went about. The newspapers began to print strange statistics that during 1924 600 disappearances had been reported, most of them young boys between 14 and 18 years of age. Next Sunday hundreds of people from Hanover and its suburbs came and stationed themselves all day on the banks of the Leine, scanning the dark river curiously. The police decided to dredge the river. On the same day 500 human bones were found. According to the medical report these had belonged to at least twenty-two different bodies, most of them young boys and men. Meanwhile, by his own audacity, the supposed author of these things, Fritz Haarmann, had been arrested.

This came about in an interesting way. After the June findings of bones, suspicion fell—at last—on Haarmann. But it was thought necessary to wait and catch him red-handed. For this the Chief of Police thought it necessary, seeing the position of the man, to send to Berlin for two detectives with whom Haarmann was not personally acquainted. These two watched him at the Railway Station. During the night of 22nd June, Haarmann was there prowling among the sleeping men. At two o'clock a quarrel burst out suddenly between him and a youngster named Fromm, a heavy stupid fellow. Haarmann rushed up to the police-post and asked them to take Fromm in charge for travelling without a ticket. Fromm then simultaneously charged Haarmann with indecency, and the screaming couple were both taken to the central station by the Berlin detectives. The opportunity was taken at last to visit Haarmann's room in the Red Row thoroughly and critically, with the result that a quantity of clothing and small objects was discovered, the material evidence for the twenty-four charges that were later made against him. He explained this as the stock of his second-hand trade, and the numerous and extensive bloodstains as the consequence of his illicit butcher's business. But assisted by another accident—the identification of the coat of the son of Haarmann's landlady by the mother of one of the victims—and pressed by an exasperated public opinion, the police put Haarmann through the 'third degree' and succeeded in extorting a confession from him. In this he accused Grans as instigator and accomplice, being at the time on bad terms with the young man; Grans' arrest followed.

Now Haarman and the State must face each other; it is not too high a thing for the murderer, nor too low for the State. They are long acquaintances: Haarmann has not to fear new judges, who can repudiate past dealings; by beautiful continuity old Germany has left intact its judges as well as its police, and its murderers, to its successor Republic. There is no repudiation of the *social* debt. Of the opponents Haarmann is the least disturbed. Not he, but his judges, feverishly try to hurry and hide: they pack the court, burk witnesses, and, that failing, expel the only independent journalist who has escaped their scrutiny at the doors, Theodor Lessing, for daring to comment upon the evidence. The central Government is mindful of its own; it followed the trial by banning most printed accounts of it for sale in the bookshops. Haarmann has no such prejudices to hamper him. He follows the pattern of all his predecessors in the gloomy throne of the dock; he is as punctilious as Landru, as impersonally fascinated by legal points as Smith, as proud as Troppmann, as unconscious as Burke, as dreadfully nervous of any evidence that reminds of the personality of his victims as any other of these unrealists. By a stupendous twist of the imagination, which shows what forces of self-deception are in him, he, the cannibal, had woven a sentimental romance round himself, with willows and keepsaking and a stylized broken heart. With a real tremor in his voice he tells them all in court: 'I want to be executed on the market-place. On my tombstone must be put this inscription: "Here lies Mass-Murderer Haarmann." On my birthday, Hans Grans must come and lay a wreath upon it.' The State judges listen to this wonderful poem in silence. It is clear that they are deferent to Haarmann; they are in his hands. He is the honest, simple man; they the tricksters, who mean by tact to stop his mouth. Haarmann and Grans stand side by side; sometimes it seems as if they forget the court to act intimate scenes as if they were free and alone. Haarmann rages, begs, cries, threatens, promises his companion, who like a stone figure looks superciliously in front of him and does not deign to turn to his old friend. In these scenes the court is also clearly with Haarmann. It joins its arguments to his, to make Grans confess. The youngster answers them in the same negligent quiet tone that he uses to his partner. But if Haarmann says he is guilty, it must be the truth. All that Haarmann says is accepted. In this atmosphere, a faintly fawning trust, we see the last unfolding of his character. He grows daily more good-tempered, and there comes on him an authority and a manner that he never had, even as a night detective. He rules the proceedings as if by moral right. To an awkward or timid witness, he administers encouragement or rebuke. 'Now, come on, you must tell us all that you know. We are here to hear the truth.' The judges nod assent. When Haarmann rebukes a witness because he allowed his son to go in rags, the court nods assent. When Haarmann denies a charge (he denied two) they nod their heads and tell the jury to acquit him of it. They accept everything: Haarmann's opinion that he is not mad, Haarmann's stilted regrets, Haarmann's charge against his companion. It is as if a secret cowed these old Hanoverian judges. It is said that they were afraid that Haarmann's full relationship to the police would be brutally blabbed. Once his time for speaking is over they play on him a sly trick; his defender, chosen by the court, makes no defence at all, and contents himself with telling the court of his loathing for his client. No rebutting medical evidence is brought.

So Haarmann politely bears his doom: decapitation. In that he feels, he is told, he pays all accounts. Grans is condemned to life imprisonment.[1] Grans takes it as indifferently as if it were an opinion on the weather. The logical riddle of finding a point—Responsibility—in the endless chain of cause and effect is, as always, but with

[1]Afterwards revised and reduced.

more intellectual meanness than usual, solved in a sentence. A judge cannot condemn himself; from every trial the State, the Collectivity, must go scot-free. But in the horrible life-cycle of a Haarmann, accomplished from larva to death's head in the very veins of the body-politic, it is a *tour de force* so lightly to decide where action begins and is decapitated, where influence ends and is excused. The unnatural marriage of his parents, the corruption of a town, which he did not invent, the asylum that allowed a homicide to escape, the science and the revenge that would not send him back again, the army that taught him the theory of manslaughter, the prison that gave him bad dreams, the enthronement of his like over the economic system in consequence of the war, the police that gave him licence and power: for none of these things is Haarmann responsible, even in the ambiguous arithmetic of Law. Take them from the crime, and what remains of Haarmann? As much as is left of Smith, without the institution of property, or of Burke without his doctors. That is, an unformed lump of clay, ugly as all that is primitive: that might well on another wheel be worked to some trifling figurine, which neither admiration nor horror could pick out of the innumerable millions of common replicas that have been cut in ephemeral attitudes of love, hate, and suffering, since the world began. Thus, strip by strip, could be removed from these ghastly bugbears that have stood before our bar—the ghoul Burke; that sullen abomination, young Troppmann; the livid Smith; Landru the thug, and this werewolf of Hanover—with their mountainous trappings that give them such an air, their huge blank masks. Until, from what they seemed, presences from a monstrous world more evil and powerful than ours, they would shrink in bulk and mystery, and when the last cloth was off, dwindle to homunculi, perhaps no bigger, no wickeder, no redder even, than new-born babies, kicking and screaming to have their will: the not-to-be-disowned children of our accursed familiar race, whose pedigee records, not only blond Abel, but the damned fraternal strain of Cain.

A Note about
the Production
of This Book

The typeface for the text of this special edition of *Murder for Profit* is Times Roman, a 20th Century design notable for its simplicity and versatility. The type was set by Arrow Composition, Inc., of Worcester, Massachusetts, and printed by The Safran Printing Company of Detroit, Michigan. The binding was done by J. W. Clement Co. of Buffalo, New York. The cover was printed by Livermore and Knight Co., a division of Printing Corporation of America, in Providence, Rhode Island.

x

The paper, TIME Reading Text, is from The Mead Corporation, Dayton, Ohio. The cover stock is from The Plastic Coating Corp., Holyoke, Massachusetts.